Creativi  or Managers

 Univers

To my parents, and particularly the memory of my father

Creativity and Innovation for Managers

Brian Clegg

Published in association with the Institute of Management

ELSEVIER
BUTTERWORTH
HEINEMANN

chartered

management

institute

AMSTERDAM • BOSTON • HEIDELBERG • LONDON • NEW YORK • OXFORD
PARIS • SAN DIEGO • SAN FRANCISCO • SINGAPORE • SYDNEY • TOKYO

Elsevier Butterworth Heinemann
Linacre House, Jordan Hill, Oxford OX2 8DP
200 Wheeler Road, Burlington, MA 01803

First published 1999
Reprinted 2001
Transferred to digital printing 2004

British Library Cataloguing in Publication Data
A catalogue record for this book is available from the British Library

ISBN 0 7506 4255 6

For information on all Elsevier Butterworth-Heinemann
publications visit our website at www.bh.com

Printed and bound in Great Britain by Lightning Source UK Ltd

Contents

Preface   vii

1   Innovation in brief   1

2   Innovation emerges   8

3   The mechanics of innovation   16

4   The innovation powerhouses   30

5   Swamps and alligators   57

6   A moment's pause   72

7   Innovation in context   79

8   Innovation SWOT   88

9   Innovation agenda   92

10 Finding out more   103

Index   109

Preface

There is probably no business discipline more subject to 'do as I say, not as I do' than creativity. A survey of major US companies taken in the mid-1990s found that 80 per cent of firms said that innovation was important to their business, while only 4 per cent thought they did it well. This disparity is frightening, but probably not surprising.

Michael Porter of Harvard Business School in his classic book, *Competitive Advantage* (Free Press, 1998), defined three ways to achieve competitive advantage: differentiation, cost-cutting and finding a niche market. Each of these vehicles depends on creativity to work effectively. Differentiation requires new approaches to products and services to make a company significantly different from the competition. Effective cost-cutting is equally dependent on creativity. The ideal, after all, is to cut costs while improving quality – a problem that certainly requires creative thought. Anyone can do 'easy' cost reduction, giving it little if any competitive value. The trick is to manage cost reductions that the opposition cannot cope with – a creative requirement if ever there was one. The niche strategy also stands or falls on creativity – to establish the right niche, and to maximize fit.

This book is designed to provide a clear picture of innovation in business. It will show how organized business creativity has originated, how it works and, most importantly, how it can be managed effectively for the benefit of the business. It will give you a quick briefing on an important management discipline without the need for in-depth study.

There is probably no subject where brevity is more relevant than creativity. The times when creativity is most called for are the times when it is most difficult to take a step back from the action. Too often, managing a business problem is like building a dam by hand. It could be done much quicker and more effectively with a spade, but it is difficult to tear yourself away to make the journey to the tool shed. Similarly, it can be hard to put a business problem to one side for long enough to bring creativity techniques to bear. This briefing will help you make the decision more logically.

Chapter 1

Innovation in brief

An overview of what creativity and innovation is, and what it can do for you, at both individual and company levels. This chapter explores ways to enhance creativity, and concludes with maps of the rest of the book.

What are creativity and innovation?

'More than a few of today's [management] theories actually imply strangling creativity and suppressing zest at a time when they've become the prime creators of economic value.' *Tom Peters, business writer and consultant*

Creativity and innovation are words that you cannot avoid. Whether you are listening to an arts programme on the radio, a politician urging a state service to get more done with less money or a keynote speech at a business conference, you will hear 'creativity' and 'innovation' bandied about. In practically every case, creativity will be seen as something good, something to be desired. Perhaps only when it comes to accounting is creativity a dirty word. Yet creativity and innovation are classic examples of concepts that everyone has a feel for but few can actually describe.

One of the problems with defining creativity is that it is not a single thing. Arthur Koestler, a key thinker in the development of an understanding of creativity, divides the creative process into three different persona: the jester, the sage and the artist. The artist represents the most traditional picture of creativity, whether composing music, writing or working in the visual arts. The sage has traditionally been the scientific and philosophical thinker, the picture of creativity which has most influenced business, typified by the sudden explosion of a new idea. The jester provides an aspect of creativity with which neither art nor business are truly comfortable. Both the arts and business take themselves very seriously, often to the extent of appearing po-faced. Yet humour is a powerful weapon for creativity. The persona Koestler chose here is very apt – the court jester was the only one who could question the decisions of the monarch, but by doing it with humour he managed to make a practical point and avoid causing offence.

From a business viewpoint, all three of Koestler's persona are important in defining creativity. From the origins of the words themselves, innovation would seem to be about newness, while creativity is about bringing something into being. A business that is to reap the benefits of creativity needs the humour of the jester to challenge the way things have always been done, the inspiration of the sage to come up with new products and services and to crack difficult business problems, and the clarity of view of the artist to refine the ideas and ensure a good fit with the real business.

Arguably there is a subtle difference between creativity and innovation. Harvard Business School's Theodore Levitt defined creativity as *thinking up* new things, while innovation was *doing* new things, but this does not really match the common usage of the words. Often, *innovation* is applied to idea generation (presumably because of its roots in 'newness'), particularly around products, while *creativity* incorporates both innovation and the task of problem-solving. Of course it is never that simple, as arguably creative problem-solving is all about generating new ideas (to solve problems), and idea generation is simply solving the problem of getting a new idea (or product or whatever). In this book the two terms will be used interchangeably with no particular weighting intended.

What can innovation do for my company?

'Now here, you see, it takes all the running you can do, to keep in the same place. If you want to get somewhere else, you must run at least twice as fast as that.' Lewis Carroll, *Through the Looking Glass*

The simple fact is that innovation can make the difference between survival and disaster. We live in a world of technological upheaval and business turmoil. The influences on business success have never been more complex. Whether your company is being buffeted by a recession halfway around the world or challenged by an unexpected newcomer, there is no room for complacency.

Competition, growing customer expectations, global/local considerations, changing workforces, exploding information resources – a barrage of business problems and imperatives, each demanding a fresh idea. Change is ever present, and it is not going to go away; it is going to get faster. There is no returning to the old days. Turmoil is not a temporary hitch in an otherwise smooth business environment, it *is* the business environment. If you can make your company innovative, you have the best possible chance of riding those business problems, coming up with great new products and services, countering the competition and surprising your customers by exceeding, not just meeting, their demands. If you can *keep* your company innovative – even more of a challenge – you can maintain this position of stability in a world of turmoil. Of course it is not the old sort of stability where nothing ever changes. This is the new stability where change is a constant, the stability of a gyroscope on a pitching platform, keeping the company on the level while everything moves around it. The quote from Lewis Carroll at the start of this section is probably the most quoted extract from a hugely quoted book, yet the Red Queen's remark has never before been quite so accurate.

Doing it differently

The Italian clothing firm Benetton is often in the news for its daring advertising, but this inclination not to run with the herd should not be a surprise. Benetton became a success by doing things differently. Ignoring the traditional approach of following fashion trends, Benetton decided to follow their customers. By producing neutral coloured clothes, then dyeing them afterwards, Benetton could react incredibly quickly to customer demand. Benetton shops are oriented to colour – even their advertising stresses this.

Benetton's example is a good one, because creativity actually created a new gap in a highly competitive marketplace. Of course one good idea will not last a business a lifetime. If Benetton is to remain successful, it will need a steady flow of new ideas. This is one of the prime benefits of systematic creativity – moving from good ideas as an occasional random occurrence to good ideas as the outcome of a simple, predictable process.

The benefits of innovation continue at the micro level. In a company where creativity is not actively encouraged, front-line employees will feel restrained by the system. They will not offer the best customer service because it will be 'more than my job's worth'. They will follow the rules. The trouble is, that great customer service is about going outside the rules where necessary. Of course there have to be guiding principles, but front-line staff need the discretion to vary from the norm to satisfy a customer. If creativity is accepted as a fundamental tenet of the company, the staff will do whatever is required to get the job done – a whole different world to the traditional approach to work. Best of all, it is win-win-win. The company does better, the customer is happier and the employees get more out of their jobs.

What does innovation mean for me?

'No matter what business you're in, your future will be shaped, even determined by innovation occurring today.' *Michael Michalko, creativity consultant*

Creativity and innovation are just as important at a personal level as they are for the company as a whole. There are very few business occupations where a level of creativity is not important. Occasionally the nature of the job means that such creativity has to be very specifically channelled – an airline pilot would not be thanked for devising innovative ways of flying a plane – but the time when it was possible to have a 'solid' career by being unimaginative are gone.

Making your company more creative gives it a better chance for success; making yourself more creative enhances both your career prospects and your potential for enjoyment of what you are doing. Innovation is no longer optional.

It may be that you already consider yourself a very innovative person. If so, there is always room for improvement. It may be, on the other hand, that you think of innovation as being the remit of someone else, the 'creatives' who you take out of their box, point at a problem, get a solution and then tidy away again before they can do any damage. Such an approach may have been good enough in the past, but it will not be in the future. Creativity is not a side issue, it is a central tenet of business survival.

Can we do anything about it?

> 'Business creativity makes the difference between success and failure. It is needed both in finding new ways to earn revenue and in finding new ways of cutting costs. It is the spur to meeting one's core business goals. It is the fuel additive that powers the engines of industry to peak performance.' *Keith Rapley, Innovation Manager, British Airways*

The requirement for creativity may be solidly established, but the knowledge of this is nothing more than an irritation if there is no vehicle for delivering creativity. For a long time it was assumed that creativity was something an individual was born with. The only way to get creativity into a company was to go out and buy it. Fortunately, while it is certainly true that individuals have vastly differing levels of creativity, anyone can have their creativity enhanced to a considerable extent. Since the 1960s a range of techniques have been developed to improve individual and group creativity. Combined with a new approach to institutionalizing innovation, these techniques can transform a company's innovative potential.

This book does not aim to make you an expert in these creativity techniques. There are plenty of other books on the market to do that – see Chapter 10 for more details. However, a knowledge of what the techniques are and what they can do, combined with a consideration of the way that an organization can change to make creativity a central part of its culture and operation are essentials to making something happen.

The maps

'Where you stumble, there your treasure lies.' Joseph Campbell, writer on myth and ancient wisdom

This book has a contents section, so why bother with anything more? Figures 1.1 and 1.2 are maps to the book – the first arranged by concept, the second the structure of the book itself. Like any business book, it is liable to be dipped into as much as it is read through from cover to cover. These maps will help with that dipping.

Content by concept

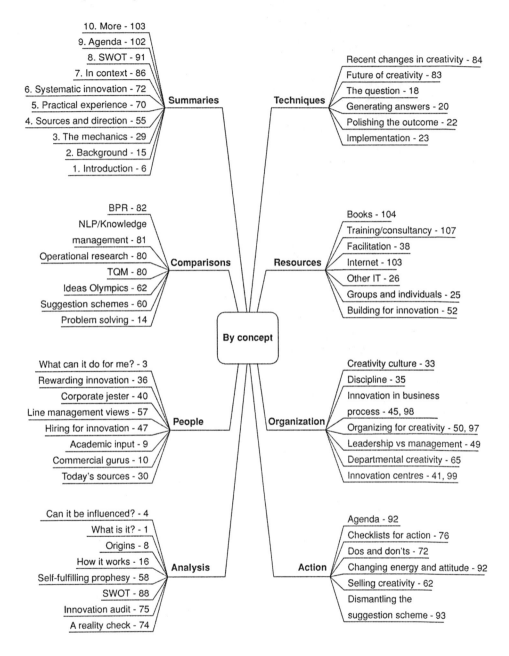

10. More - 103
9. Agenda - 102
8. SWOT - 91
7. In context - 86
6. Systematic innovation - 72
5. Practical experience - 70   **Summaries**
4. Sources and direction - 55
3. The mechanics - 29
2. Background - 15
1. Introduction - 6

Techniques
Recent changes in creativity - 84
Future of creativity - 83
The question - 18
Generating answers - 20
Polishing the outcome - 22
Implementation - 23

BPR - 82
NLP/Knowledge
management - 81
Operational research - 80
TQM - 80   **Comparisons**
Ideas Olympics - 62
Suggestion schemes - 60
Problem solving - 14

Resources
Books - 104
Training/consultancy - 107
Facilitation - 38
Internet - 103
Other IT - 26
Groups and individuals - 25
Building for innovation - 52

By concept

What can it do for me? - 3
Rewarding innovation - 36
Corporate jester - 40
Line management views - 57   **People**
Hiring for innovation - 47
Academic input - 9
Commercial gurus - 10
Today's sources - 30

Organization
Creativity culture - 33
Discipline - 35
Innovation in business
process - 45, 98
Organizing for creativity - 50, 97
Leadership vs management - 49
Departmental creativity - 65
Innovation centres - 41, 99

Can it be influenced? - 4
What is it? - 1
Origins - 8
How it works - 16   **Analysis**
Self-fulfilling prophesy - 58
SWOT - 88
Innovation audit - 75
A reality check - 74

Action
Agenda - 92
Checklists for action - 76
Dos and don'ts - 72
Changing energy and attitude - 92
Selling creativity - 62
Dismantling the
suggestion scheme - 93

Figure 1.1 Content of book by concept

Content by chapter

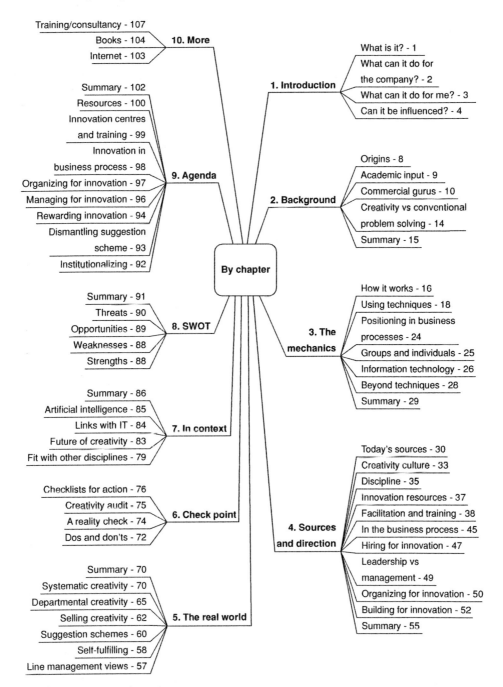

Figure 1.2 Content of book by chapter

Chapter 2

Innovation emerges

This chapter looks at the origins of creativity in a general sense, and the specifics of business creativity. It considers how the work of the pioneers was given a commercial workover by gurus like Edward de Bono and Roger von Oech. It examines the differences that establish creativity as a separate discipline from traditional problem-solving.

The birth of creativity

> 'Looking at the brain's structure of axons and neurons, one can imagine that new ideas are combinations of existing ones.' *Chan Bok*
> — *developer of the Axon Idea Processor*

Where did creativity come from? This is a bit like asking how long is a piece of string. As long as there have been people, there have been creative people and there has been creativity. Equally, that creativity has been applied both to what could loosely be described as art and what might be thought of as 'practical' creativity – the forerunner of business creativity – innovation with a specific, beneficial end in mind, rather than creativity for its own sake.

At any time in history there have been creative people around. Whether we consider Archimedes' leap of imagination in the bath, the elegant solutions to the combination of space and weight that marked the medieval stonemason's craft, Leonardo da Vinci's eclectic skills or the vast outpouring of Victorian ingenuity, creativity has been a common thread. Until the 1900s, though, creativity has been very much thought of as a gift. An inherent ability, rather than something that could be taught or improved on. As with so many other things, the legacy of the twentieth century has been to put the assumptions of the past into a different perspective.

The academics arrive

'If at first the idea is not absurd, then there is no hope for it.'
Albert Einstein

Throughout the twentieth century, scientists and philosophers struggled with the nature of thought and mind. But the breakthrough as far as business creativity was concerned was the work of Alex Osborn. Osborn took creativity away from the theoreticians and moved it into applied science. Osborn's central tenet was that at any one time we have a very limited view of what we actually know. As we go through life we accumulate a vast amount of experience and influence, hardly any of which is consciously available to us. However, this does not mean that all this knowledge is inaccessible – merely that something has to be done to gain access to it.

That, however, Osborn argues, is only the start of the problem. Our natural tendency is to filter and check out ideas as they come up. It is an entirely natural act to evaluate and discard anything that is apparently useless or irrelevant. This tendency extends beyond our own thoughts. We are just as happy – in fact probably more happy – to pass judgement on the ideas of others. The result is that creativity is powerfully suppressed. When ideas are new, almost everyone can be crushed by premature judgement. Osborn pointed out the need to hold back from evaluation, both to allow ideas to be refined and to prevent participants from suppressing their own ideas before they are even mentioned, for fear of being made to look silly.

Premature evaluation
It is hard to overemphasize the dangers of evaluating ideas too early. Consider how easy it would be to squash the following ideas or inventions in their early stages:
- a glue that does not stick properly
- a painkiller made from tree bark
- eating a food cooked which is poisonous when uncooked (kidney beans)
- a tape recorder that does not record, which you can wear
- democracy
- horseless carriages.

Osborn's great contribution to business creativity, to try to overcome this tendency, was brainstorming. The idea was simple. By having free association of ideas and no criticism or judgement allowed, a much richer source of creative input would be possible. Brainstorming caught the imagination of consultants and academics alike, and became a standard business tool. Unfortunately, it is not enough on its own. It only addresses the second of Osborn's points. When done properly, brainstorming overcomes the inclination to evaluate. However, it does nothing to tap into the deep well of creative possibility which most of us have hidden away.

Osborn was well aware of this, and proposed a series of mechanisms to penetrate into the creative depths. Almost all the creativity techniques which have since been popularized can be traced back to Osborn's mechanisms. These include:

- adaptation – modification – substitution
- addition
- subtraction
- rearrangement
- reversal
- combination.

Unlike brainstorming, though, these concepts were a little too theoretical in Osborn's work to capture the public imagination, and it was not until they were taken up by the gurus of business creativity that they became more widely used.

If Osborn provided the logic that was going to make creativity a practical business tool, Arthur Koestler provided the soul. Koestler had a remarkable background as foreign correspondent and novelist before becoming interested in science and the mind. In 1964 he published *The Act of Creation* (Penguin Arkana, 1989) which was to be the other pillar on which creativity as a management science could be established. Osborn had produced pragmatic tools; Koestler had provided a thoughtful basis to underpin them. It now only required the right personalities to push creativity to the forefront.

Gurus and commerce

'The world might be going global, but there are many, many fragments of markets to explore. Markets are moving and changing so fast. Opportunities come by so quickly and can be missed. The **only** culture guaranteed to spot and deliver on these fast moving windows (more like keyholes) is a creative one – where flexibility, speed of response, intelligent response, passionate follow-through and theatrical-like fervour to deliver right up to the final curtain are what's needed to get the job done.' *Mark Adams, Director, Text 100 plc*

The line between academics and commerce is rarely as thin as it is in the world of creativity. Go into a bookshop and hunt for the works of Edward de Bono and you are just as likely to find them in the Psychology section as in the Business section.

Yet there is no doubt that between the 1960s and the 1980s, the era when creativity first became an explicitly desirable commodity, that there was a conscious move into creativity as a commercial discipline. Two names stand out strongest as the gurus of commercial creativity from this period: Edward de Bono and Roger von Oech.

Edward de Bono

De Bono's approach to creativity is a very cerebral one. There is nothing strange or unconventional about de Bono. Instead he concentrates on creativity as an intellectual discipline and a business tool. Even the titles of de Bono's books – *Serious Creativity* (HarperCollins, 1996), for example – echo this feel. De Bono has, in fact, criticized those who feel that fun ought to be central to creativity. There is no doubt that he has a point. It has sometimes been true that a creativity practitioner has thought it enough to be crazy and unorthodox, and that such an approach is not particularly helpful. Equally, some executives are uncomfortable with fun in the workplace. But there is also a danger of making creativity so serious that it becomes dull, and suffers as a result.

De Bono's biggest contributions to practical innovation are probably lateral thinking, 'six thinking hats', creativity in schools and pinstriped creativity.

Lateral thinking

The term 'lateral thinking', now widely associated with the process of innovation, was coined by Edward de Bono. This concept of dealing with an intractable problem by coming at it from a totally different direction may not be original, but no one has rivalled de Bono in raising awareness of the approach.

In two early books, de Bono popularized the concept (*Lateral Thinking*, Penguin, 1990) and gave readers practice at thinking laterally (*The Five Day Course in Thinking*, Pelican, 1969). His definitive book on creativity, *Serious Creativity*, is subtitled 'Using the power of lateral thinking to create new ideas', and is the bedrock of much of the psychological/logical school of creativity.

Six thinking hats

Arguably de Bono's most original contribution to business, 'six thinking hats' provides an alternative to the confrontational approach to meetings and discussion. Just as there are two approaches to justice – the adversarial system seen in UK and US courts, and the inquisitorial system in many continental European courts – so there are two ways of running a meeting. Many such gatherings are adversarial, with each member out to put their own point but uninterested in the contributions of others. Six thinking hats provides a means of moving out of this adversarial approach and into a more constructive one.

Six thinking hats breaks the discussion process down into six clear roles or approaches, each identified by a different coloured hat to aid memory. By explicitly running a group in a single mode at any one time, de Bono argues that it is possible to reduce the energy wasted on adversarial input and concentrate on constructive input. For example, when working with 'yellow hats on', the group can only consider positive contributions, minimizing conflict.

Six thinking hats is a pragmatically effective technique – it can be seen to work with very little effort. Usually the biggest problem in using it is overcoming initial resistance to the idea of the hats themselves. De Bono went on to develop a parallel process in 'six action shoes', but this has significantly less original content.

Creativity in schools

It is a frightening fact that creativity and schools have traditionally had a very poor fit. In part this is due to the nature of the education process. Creativity is not ideal when the main aim of education is to provide the answer required by the examination. Generally, the educational system assumes that there is a single right answer to a problem (that expected by the teacher or examiner), and aims not to develop new, innovative solutions. In fact, if anything, education is a positive brake on creativity. Children go into secondary education with a surprisingly high level of creative thinking, and come out much less effective.

Edward de Bono has not only recognized this problem, but has also done something about it. His CoRT (Cognitive Research Trust) programme is specifically designed to help school students develop creative thinking skills. The concept of teaching children how to be creative is quite alien to the UK and US education systems, but has considerable popularity now (often thanks to de Bono) in Australia and other Pacific Rim countries. It is a shame that there has been less penetration of the concept in Europe and the USA. After all, no one would be expected to operate a complex, unlabelled piece of machinery without some training. It is stunning that most educational establishments take the 'how to' of using your brain as a given.

Pinstriped creativity

This is my term, rather than de Bono's own, but highlights an important aspect of his work – making creativity acceptable at a senior level in companies. Traditionally, any analytical or decision-making technique has had best penetration at middle levels in a company, where most day-to-day decision-making and problem-solving occurs. De Bono commands a high level of respect which has resulted in considerable penetration into areas of senior management, including his Creativity Forum programme, which brings together executives from corporate organizations to discuss and practise creativity.

Roger von Oech

'The human body has two ends on it: one to create with and one to sit on. Sometimes people get their ends reversed. When this happens they need a kick in the seat of the pants.'   *Roger von Oech*

If de Bono is at the summit of intellectual business creativity, Roger von Oech rides high in the pop culture of innovation. This is not to say that von Oech is of the school de Bono has criticized for being all fun and no content – von Oech's approach is very practical – but that von Oech presents creativity techniques with Californian pizzazz and no stuffiness. It is probably not surprising, then, that von Oech has become the preferred guru of the Silicon Valley and much of the USA.

To see the difference between de Bono and von Oech, it is necessary to go no further than the terms used for a mechanism to force someone into a different viewpoint. De Bono applies to this an invented word 'po', which he has defined as a provocative or provoking operation. Von Oech refers to it as a whack on the side of the head. His principle books, *A Whack on the Side of the Head* (Warner, 1983) and *A Kick in the Seat of the Pants* (HarperCollins, 1986) look more like entertainment books than business books. But underneath the light presentation is a serious message.

Blockages

In *A Whack on the Side of the Head*, von Oech concentrates on the blockages to creativity. One of the tenets of effective innovation is that the best way to approach a problem is to uncover the obstacles in the way of success and fix them. In *A Whack on the Side of the Head* von Oech looks at the obstacles that get in the way of being creative and works through destroying them. This approach is probably von Oech's greatest contribution, and he puts his message across in splendid form, with a great deal of fun and side activity along the way.

Explorer, artist, judge and warrior

Von Oech's other big input was the division of the creative process into four primary activities. As we will see in Chapter 3, this approach is hardly unique, but von Oech's divisions of the explorer, the artist, the judge and the warrior are particularly evocative. These categories are explored in more depth in the follow-up book, *A Kick in the Seat of the Pants*. This may not have been such a breakthrough, but the categorization is stimulating, and the book is another impressive source. Von Oech has carried this concept forward into a pack of cards, *The Creative Whack Pack* (1989, US Games Systems, also available as a computer program). The cards can be very effective as a guide for a creativity session, providing questions to start probing a creative solution.

Creativity techniques or problem-solving

'Creativity is essential for any business. Let's suppose creativity is the capacity for generating novel and valued outputs. There is no obvious way through which a business can generate and maintain a competitive advantage without some such process. At present business practitioners and researchers alike are groping towards an understanding of factors that help or hinder creativity.' *Tudor Rickards, Professor of Creativity and Organisational Change, Manchester Business School*

Creativity techniques are a means to an end – typically solving a business problem, whether it involves devising a new product or service, or removing an obstacle to getting something done. As such, creativity techniques are not unique. There are other approaches available. However, the alternatives, like the well-established commercial Kepner-Tregoe methodology, depend primarily on analysis, breaking down the problem and applying the lessons of experience. These techniques are designed to assist with an understanding of the requirement, then to generate possible solutions based on the experience and expertise of the decision-maker.

A quick examination of a pair of traditional problem-solving methodologies will make this clear. Hill-climbing has been a popular approach for many years. The idea takes the model of climbing a hill where it is not possible to see the summit. Without a map, you will typically resort to always trying to go up hill. It will not necessarily take you to the highest summit on the hill, but it certainly will get you to a relatively high point. This approach to problem-solving breaks down the problem, looking for a positive first step, then reassessing the direction from that point. For example, I might approach the problem of getting a book published by breaking it down to writing a proposal, sending it to publishers, writing the book and correcting the proofs. When I have written the proposal and sent it off, I have taken two positive uphill steps. Of course, it may be a false summit. I could get no positive reply, in which case I will have to take a different route to my destination.

Another approach is to attempt to minimize the difference between the present state and the solution, reducing the problem to a lesser difficulty. For example, if my problem was to produce a brochure for my company, I might decide to take on a professional printer who can put the whole thing together for me. Now I have reduced the problem to locating a good printer.

There is nothing wrong with these methods. In fact, such step-by-step or analytical techniques often provide a good way of solving a problem. Yet increasingly they are not enough. The combination of competitive pressure and collapsing timescales calls for a more radical solution to business problems, a more original idea for new product development. The benefit that creativity techniques bring is in forcing the decision-maker out of the well trodden path, giving a totally different perspective which is impossible from an analytical technique, based on the current situation and on history.

Executive summary

- A move of perspective from pure artistic creativity to practical creativity.
- Alex Osborn devised brainstorming and identified both the need to stimulate access to the hidden depths of the brain and the need to prevent filtering and censorship of new ideas before they can be built on and refined.
- Edward de Bono built on Osborn's ideas with the concept of lateral thinking, the six thinking hats meeting/discussion process, creativity in schools and 'serious' business creativity.
- Roger von Oech built on Osborn's ideas by making creativity fun (again), concentrating on removing the blockages to creativity and expanding the creative armoury.
- Creativity is different from conventional problem-solving techniques as it moves away from analysis and the lessons of experience, recognizing that these cannot produce innovation. Competitive pressures and collapsing timescales call for something more – the stimulation to innovate that creativity techniques can give.

Chapter 3

The mechanics of innovation

This book is not a course in creativity, nor an exploration of the workings of the mind, yet some understanding of the forces at work and the basic workings of creativity techniques are essential in considering the best approach to take. This chapter goes into the practicalities of creativity, the impact of information technology and the possibility of going beyond techniques to something more internalized.

How does it work?

'Creativity is like a bend in a straight road – the dull driver will never know it's there until too late; the well prepared driver is the one who uses it as the overtaking opportunity. It is far more fun driving fast than safely, and you get there quicker too.' *Ian Campbell, Financial Services Manager*

Fascinating though the study of creativity may be, the purpose of this book is to gain practical insights. In asking how creativity techniques work, we are interested less in the biology and psychology than the pragmatic linkages to outcomes.

With this brief in mind, creativity is needed when something new is required. The very term 'innovation' incorporates the Latin word for new. If an existing solution, an existing product or an existing approach would do, there would be no need for creativity. We could carry on the way we always had. As the old saying has it, 'if it ain't broke, don't fix it'. The need for creativity is stimulated by the fact that 'it' is broken – or increasingly that it is not broken yet, but it will be if no action is taken.

For true innovation, simple experience is not enough to come up with an answer. Experience depends on the way things have been done before.

Innovation calls for a different approach. As Osborn pointed out, we are sitting on an immense collection of resources that do not usually emerge. Creativity techniques open up this collection. At their most basic, this is done by sleight of hand. We misdirect the conscious, so the unconscious can get to work. Everyone has done this when trying to remember something. Put the problem to one side, think of something completely different and the answer will pop up. Similarly this 'put it to one side' approach can generate fresh thinking, but it is not a particularly forceful technique.

The vast majority of creativity techniques positively plunge us into the reservoir of ideas, rather than using misdirection and hoping something will float out. Techniques are short activities which force those concerned to think in a different way – perhaps by distorting the problem itself. The techniques may give the solver a totally different viewpoint. They may step away from the problem and make a direct attack on the idea pool. But whichever approach is taken, creativity techniques will attempt to tie the problem to unexpected parts of the individual or group knowledge base in order to gain new insights and possibilities.

Self-patterning systems

A number of writers on creativity, particularly Edward de Bono, have pointed out the significance of the mind as a self-patterning system. Normally we would say that something which is logical once put in place, was also logical before it was thought up. This should make it possible to generate a creative result by logic alone. However, this argument holds true only for a static system – one where the pathways are fixed. The mind, and particularly the way ideas are generated, can be seen rather as a self-patterning system. Imagine a sloping tray of wax. A hot liquid is poured down it. The liquid melts tracks in the wax – now there is a way through for the liquid to follow, but before the passage of the liquid there was no such track. The liquid has made its own pattern. Also, the more you use the pattern, the deeper it gets.

We can see the same thing happening with an idea. Once the pattern has been established, the track can be seen. Before long the pattern has become a rut in its own right. If the idea is worthwhile, it becomes obvious after the idea has been produced that it is a logical step forward. We can follow the track back from outcome to origin. However, before the pattern was made there was no way to logically follow through. Creativity techniques often seem to produce illogical, even silly, suggestions to begin with, but that is because the pattern is yet to be established.

Alone, generating original ideas is unlikely to achieve anything. The other requirement, also identified by Osborn, is the need to prevent those involved from evaluating these ideas too soon. This requirement applies to individuals' own ideas and everyone else's. When ideas first emerge they are delicate, unformed and often silly. If we give way to the natural tendency to squash the impractical, most new ideas will be thrown out before they are fully formed. As individuals or as groups we need time to take an idea and let it mature before it can be used. For this reason creativity techniques are often best fitted into a framework that allows ideas to be generated, built on and refined before they are assessed. It is quite possible to use a standalone idea-generating technique to good effect, but for most serious applications it is more effective to consider four quick steps.

The number of steps is somewhat arbitrary, yet an amazing number of different writers on the subject have come to roughly the same conclusions – enough to make this seem a very practical approach. The earliest reference I can locate is D. M. Johnson, who identified three phases in *The Psychology of Thought* (Harper and Row, 1955). His steps – preparation, production and judgement – correspond neatly to the first three identified here. The fourth step, completing the picture, is implementation (see Figure 3.1).

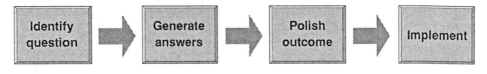

Figure 3.1 The four stages of creativity

Step 1: Identifying the question

'The most important word in promoting creativity is "let".' *Henry Berry, director of Theory B*

It might seem unnecessary to start by looking at the question. After all, if a creativity technique is to be employed, we presumably know what it is that we are looking for. The trouble is that, especially when trying to solve a problem, the requirement is often more assumption than fact. It is easy to try to fix the symptoms of a problem rather than the problem itself. This may be what is required but, if so, it should be a conscious decision rather than action taken by default.

What is more, rephrasing the problem can sometimes make a solution obvious where none was visible before. A good example of this is given by J. R. Hayes in *Cognitive Psychology* (Dorsey Press, 1978). Hayes uses a well-known puzzle involving a chessboard. The assumption is that we have a set of dominoes, each of which fits over two squares on the chessboard. We then cut off the squares from two opposite corners of the board. Is it possible to cover all the remaining squares with dominoes? The answer is no (because each domino must cover one white and one black square, yet two identically coloured squares were removed), but it is rarely obvious. However, a simple rephrasing of the question makes it entirely transparent. There are 32 couples who are to be matched up by the village matchmaker. Two men die. Can the matchmaker still match up 31 couples? Obviously not. The problem has not changed, only the problem statement.

The right question

BAA plc, the company responsible for Heathrow Airport, had a problem. Car parking brought in much less revenue than the concessionaires – shops and services within the airport. So BAA addressed itself to the problem of how to allocate space currently used for parking to concessionaires, without making access to the airport difficult. The problem seemed intractable. Someone came up with an alternative question – how to turn parking into a set of concessions attacking different segments of the market (at that time all parking was handled by a single company), and hence earn as much from parking space as from the other concessionaires. Suddenly, just by rephrasing the question, the answer was obvious. The result was a triumph for BAA – and all for asking the right question.

There are a number of techniques to help clarify the question. It will help to have a clear understanding of the facts surrounding the requirement. A quick survey of these, perhaps represented in a visual form (like the maps in Chapter 1) will help put the question into context. It is usually worth asking the question 'what if we do nothing?' There is often an assumption that something has to be done, yet the option of taking no action can be a low-cost, effective approach. Assuming something must be done, it is helpful to produce one or more statements in the form 'How to. . .' It has been found that adopting this style helps ensure that there is a clear question in mind.

Generally there will not be a single question, but several. Before proceeding with the initial formulation, it is worth looking at alternatives. One technique for doing this is to consider the obstacles. Look at the desired outcome, then establish what it is that is getting in the way of making this happen. Removing these obstacles becomes a set of objectives in its own right. Another technique that can give valuable insights is to repeatedly ask the question 'why?'

Example

We are about to have a creativity session with the question 'How to reduce packing costs by 10 per cent'. A repeated question 'why?' works as follows:

- Why do you want to reduce packing costs?
  - Because they make our products too expensive.
- Why do you want to make your products less expensive?
  - Because our competitor has similar products at a lower price.

- Why does the competitor have similar products at a lower price?
  - Because they manufacture in Eastern Europe.
- Why do they manufacture in Eastern Europe?
  - Because labour costs less there.

From this simple process we can now identify several possible questions:

- How can we make our products less expensive?
- How can we make our products different from those of our competitor?
- How can we move our manufacturing to Eastern Europe?
- How can we reduce our labour costs?

It may have been that all these options were considered before coming down to the packing cost question. If so, that's fine. But the process ensures that some consideration is given to alternatives, and will often uncover something that has been missed.

Step 2: Generating answers

'To have a great idea, have a lot of them.' *Thomas Edison, inventor, scientist and businessman*

After the initial stage there should be some questions to answer. One or more are carried forward to the second stage for action. Usually these will be the questions which are most appealing to those involved. If the outcome is not satisfactory, or there is interest in exploring further it is quite possible to return to the questions and look at several more.

It is at the answer stage that the true creativity techniques, the methods for moving the viewpoint to a different spot, are employed. There is a huge range of techniques available which it is not realistic or appropriate to detail here. For more information on techniques, see the practical business books suggested in Chapter 10.

Techniques broadly split into three main types. Some involve modifying the problem – for example, by assuming that a key attribute of the problem was not true. If we were trying to improve the profitability of a secretarial agency, we might see how this were possible if the agency did not employ any secretaries. The thoughts and ideas this generates are then fed back into the real problem. Another related approach is to modify a dimension of the problem. What if it was much bigger, or smaller, or involved a different timescale? If we were looking at ways to improve communications in a company, what would we do if we had to communicate only to one person, or to one million people. At the extreme, we can distort the problem so much that we invert it. What do we have to do to make the opposite come true? For instance, if the aim were to improve customer service, what would we do to make customer service worse? The lessons from this approach can then be applied to the real problem.

The second type of technique uses a random stimulation to push those involved away from their habitual linkages with the problem, forcing a new viewpoint. There are many possible stimuli. We might use a randomly selected word, a picture, an object, a quotation or an event from history. Whichever is used, the technique involves putting the problem to one side and first looking at what is being used as a stimulus. What is it like? What are its attributes? What does it remind us of? What associations do we have with it? These attributes and associations are then tied back to the problem itself. For example, we might be looking at devising a new household tool. Given the random word 'dolphin', we might generate associations like 'sea', 'free', 'friendly', 'splashing', 'shows', 'whale song', 'flipper', 'doing tricks', 'clicking', 'seen from a boat'. These associations are then used to help with the problem. What sort of new tool would click? Whale songs are calming – can we come up with a household item that helps people feel calm? What sort of tools might cause a splash? And so on.

The third broad category of technique makes use of something external to pull thoughts in a different direction. It could be simply a case of fantasizing – what would we do if we had a magic wand and could make anything happen? Alternatively, we can call on someone else to help. If creativity is all about getting a different viewpoint, what would someone totally unconnected with the problem area do? This technique works best by moving well away from reality. For instance, if we were trying to obtain land to expand a factory, what would a historical character like St Francis or Genghis Khan do? What would someone with a totally different job, like a surgeon or a plumber do? What would a fictional character like a starship captain or a comic-book hero do? A final example of this kind of technique is the use of metaphor. We can force a new viewpoint by insisting that an unlikely metaphor is true. What could we deduce if we say 'improving our market awareness is just like a penny farthing bicycle'? Although the metaphor is totally spurious, it is amazing how often such an approach works. The brain seems to cope with concepts by using metaphors, so forcing a metaphor can be a very effective way to make something happen.

These techniques can seem unlikely. Creativity has sometimes been described as 'uncommon sense'. If the solution was obvious, i.e. was common sense, it would have been implemented straightaway. There would have been no need for creativity. When the problem is harder, we need to move away from common sense, to come up with something different. Along the way, the approach may seem silly or strange – that does not matter, as long the ideas generated are good. Because we are dealing with uncommon sense, it is difficult to accept the validity of the techniques without actually trying them. It will often take experience to make them acceptable.

Uncommon sense

Nobel prize-winning physicist, Professor Brian Josephson of Cambridge University gives a good example of uncommon sense in action when thinking about homeopathy. Critics of this method of producing medicines by repeatedly diluting a poison, point out that there are practically no molecules of the active ingredient left, and so assume that homeopathic medicines have no use beyond the psychological. Supporters of homeopathy argue that the effect is due to modifications in the water's structure.

This may or may not be true – at first sight, a fluid like water cannot have its structure altered. But Professor Josephson points out that liquid crystals flow like an ordinary fluid, while still managing to maintain an ordered structure. Another related possible phenomenon known as 'memory of water' would have even bigger implications were it proved – but few scientists are interested in even considering it. Professor Josephson argues that the ease with which anything outside conventional thinking is dismissed by the modern scientific community shows the limited vision – lack of creativity – that is present. The professor is not suggesting we should all be gullible, but that true creativity requires an open mind – to let the idea go the distance before it is criticized. This requirement for uncommon sense is as important in business creativity as it is in the academic world.

Step 3: Polishing the outcome

'When you have two or more ideas that have nothing to do with each other you may consider them as complementaries.' *Adriano Gonzalez-Regueral, UNICEF*

A good creativity session will generate lots of ideas, many of them wild and unlikely. A wall full of flip chart paper covered in ideas can be very satisfying, but it will not lead to a successful implementation. Before the idea can be put into practice it is necessary to select something to go forward with, and to polish the idea.

Selection can be a difficult issue. Faced with a whole host of ideas, how should we proceed? Generally, the best approach is not to select on practicality, but on appeal. Which idea is the most appealing with no concern for practicality; practicality can come later. Whichever way an idea is selected, some participants in creativity sessions are worried about the remainder. What about all those other ideas? What if one is better? There are two issues to be dealt with here. It may be that some ideas are relevant to other problems – if so, it is important that they are passed on to the problem-owner. It would be a shame to waste them. If, however, these are other ideas for the same problem, they have to be put aside. They may be returned to, but the point of a creativity session is to come up with a practical idea or solution. Not to come up with every idea, or even the very best. As long as the chosen idea delivers what is required, it does not matter that there are half a dozen equally good, or even better, possibilities. This concern with the other ideas goes back to our education. So often we are looking for the one, true, right answer, where in fact there are many. It is an urge that needs suppression.

Having chosen an idea to carry forward, it now needs to be made practical. Take a few minutes to look at the good points of the idea. Only allow positive contributions. What is good about it, and how could the good points be made even better? Then look at the negative. What is wrong with the idea, and how could it be made better? By going through such a process it is possible to take what seemed a totally impractical idea (but one that was very appealing) and turn it into something that can be used, but still maintains its innovative thrust. It is much more likely that such an approach will generate an appropriate innovative solution than by selecting an idea on practicality.

Step 4: Implementation

'The way to get good ideas is to get lots of ideas and throw the bad ones away.' *Linus Pauling, Nobel prize-winning chemist*

Good implementation is as necessary for the output of a creative process as it is for any other project or task. There is nothing particularly special about a creative process in this respect, however, there is an unusual risk. Having put significant effort into generating ideas and polishing them up, there is often a temptation to think that implementation can look after itself. It has sadly been too often the case that a group has come away from a creativity session with a flip chart full of great ideas, then has done nothing further with them. Arguably, without implementation there is no creativity – an idea which is never used has no value. For this reason, it is important that planning for implementation is considered a part of the creative process, not a wholly separate exercise.

While the general need for implementation and planning remains the same however the idea was generated, it is often the case that a creative solution will be breaking new ground. This militates against planning in great detail. It is usually the case that an innovative solution will best be suited to an iterative, prototyping approach – get something together quickly, try it out and refine it – than a methodology that requires each aspect of the implementation to be planned down to the last detail and the last minute.

Realistically, the implementation plan from a creativity session should establish:

- Who – who owns the implementation and will make it happen.
- What – what resources they will need (people, physical and information).

- When – broad timescales for starting and ending.
- How – what approach will be taken; what communication is needed.
- Where – where the milestones are that measure progress.
- Help – who to call if things go wrong, and how to call them.

None of these needs be in great detail, but if they can be established for all but the most trivial implementation, the chances of success will be greatly enhanced.

Positioning creativity in business processes

'In our emerging technology company we can never stand still. The whole business has to participate in the creative process to find innovative and ingenious solutions to dynamically changing opportunities.' *Jeremy N. White, Chairman Nettec PLC*

Creativity is not normally an isolated requirement in business. Artistic creativity may be an end in itself, but business creativity will have specific aims in mind, and as such should fit with the processes of the company. We will be looking more at how to fit creativity into normal business life in Chapter 4, and in the innovation agenda in Chapter 9, but for the moment it is enough to consider where creativity is appropriate.

Bearing in mind that the prime aims of business creativity are problem-solving and idea generation, there are some key times when creativity naturally comes into play:

- **When determining strategy** – whether working in regular strategy meetings or in larger-scale off-site strategy sessions, creativity can be a powerful tool to ensure that the future direction is genuinely forward looking and original.
- **When starting a project** – at the outset of a project many variables are still unsure, and there will inevitably be problems.
- **When devising a new product or service** – the application is very direct and obvious here.
- **When a specific problem occurs** – whether it is industrial action or supply shortages, there are many problems that arise along the way. An innovative solution, quickly reached, is in great demand.

Such applications are essentially externally driven. However, creativity is a learned skill. Regular use of creativity techniques results in improved general personal creativity and improved use of the techniques when required by one of these external drivers. It therefore makes a lot of sense to have regular creativity sessions driven by the need to enhance creativity rather than a specific problem.

These regular sessions can operate at two levels. Individuals should be encouraged to have a short, regular practice session. This need take no more than 15 minutes a week. The individual takes a real problem, personal or business, and applies a creativity technique to it. If there are some useful outcomes, these can be carried forward, but the main purpose of the exercise is practice, not problem solution. Similarly, team meetings can benefit from a short, regular session, perhaps 20 minutes once a month. At this session a team member introduces a new technique to the rest of the team, who then use it together. Again, the purpose is more learning and practice than the outcome, resulting in a broader armoury of creativity techniques available when a problem is encountered.

If developing creativity is made part of the business process in this way, it will be a much more natural tool. It will no more seem odd to use a creativity technique at a strategy session than it would to use a spreadsheet or a checklist. Having the development of creativity in the process is the key to institutionalizing creativity itself.

Groups and individuals

'In the long history of mankind, those who learned to collaborate
and improvise most effectively have prevailed.' *Charles Darwin*

There are many activities that are performed better by groups or alternatively by individuals. Of late, the cult of the team has meant that the individualist has had a hard time of it. Compare the feelings associated with the descriptions 'loner' and 'team player'. Creativity is heavily dependent on individual input. A group cannot have an idea, only an individual is capable of this. This can immediately make creativity suspect.

However, while it is true that many well-formed ideas can be generated by a single individual, creativity is not just about idea generation. The best creativity takes an idea, builds on it, perhaps combines it with one or more other ideas and refines it out of all recognition. All these activities work particularly effectively in a group. By bringing together the experience and knowledge of a range of people, most ideas can be improved.

Of course, there is the saying that 'a camel is a horse designed by committee'. A group may not only improve an idea, but also hang so much extra burden on it as to make it entirely useless. Similarly, an individual can become so enthused by an impractical idea that he or she holds on to it long past its practical value.

Getting the best return out of creative effort requires an acknowledgement of the differences between individual and group input. The individual nature of idea generation should make it obvious that it is valuable to respect and nurture the ability of individuals to provide input of ideas on business problems. When a creativity session is underway it is best if individuals are first given the opportunity to generate ideas individually. This runs counter to the way brainstorming is often used, but is much more likely to achieve original ideas.

If a group is available, it can best contribute after the initial idea generation stage. We will be looking later at ways of institutionalizing creativity and bringing it to different groups. It is enough for the moment to be aware of this key difference between groups and individuals, and of the need where possible to foster both approaches.

Information technology

'The greatest stimulus to creativity is finding oneself having to write a progress report and then realizing that you have consumed more than the budgeted resources while regressing against the plan.' *Bob Malcolm, director, Ideo Limited*

Computers and creativity seem uncomfortable bedfellows at first. Combining the mechanical, inhuman efficiency of a computer with the unpredictable, human spark of creativity seems impossible. Yet this imagined conflict ignores the nature of creativity techniques. They are themselves mechanical. Bearing in mind that a technique is simply a means of releasing a human being's hidden resources, it becomes less unlikely that information technology (IT) can contribute to creativity. In fact it has a significant role to play, increasingly so as communications become more effective.

At the most basic level, the computer is a support resource for human creativity. Whether it is providing a vehicle for writing a business proposal or a source of information giving background to a problem area, the computer is a natural tool. But there is more that it can contribute. Everyday computer software can be used to support creativity techniques; the World Wide Web can be both a research tool and a direct source of creative stimulation; electronic mail and bulletin boards can improve group creativity and there is an increasing range of software available specifically designed to enhance creativity.

Use of everyday software to support techniques generally revolves around generation of a stimulus. Most creativity techniques depend on using a distracting stimulus to move the individual's viewpoint, giving them an opportunity to see the problem and the solution in a different way. Many of these techniques use a random stimulus – and randomness is a natural ability for the computer. The spellchecker in a word processor can be used to generate random key words by entering nonsense and checking it. The thesaurus can provide chained words, starting from a key word about the problem area and linking on to alternatives. Perhaps most effectively, random typing into the contents box of an electronic encyclopaedia will turn up an unpredictable article which can be used to provide starting points for new ideas.

The World Wide Web (the Web) is probably the single most important tool for supporting creativity. Where once it was an unstructured collection of useless information it is now an unmatched repository of knowledge. Admittedly it is still unstructured, and still contains plenty of garbage, but the volume of useful information is now overwhelming. This makes the Web ideal both as a general creativity stimulant – 5 minutes' random browsing can spark all sorts of new ideas – and as a source of further information on creativity. See Chapter 10 for more details on creativity on the Web. Web sites can also provide a similar technique support to an encyclopaedia by using a 'cool site of the day' or similar feature to access an effectively random, but guaranteed interesting site. Within a company, an intranet – in effect a private web – can often extend the value of the Web by taking internal communications from being the traditional, stultified corporate communications of the in-house magazine to being something lively and vibrant. Provided anyone in the company can publish on the intranet through simple means (not necessarily uncontrolled, but unbureaucratic) the intranet can foster two-way communication and fuel creativity in a company that has the right culture.

Electronic mail and bulletin boards (whether Internet based like newsgroups, or proprietary like Lotus Notes) can contribute a great deal to group creativity. While it is usually best to gather a group together for creative input, it is not always practical. These indirect means can be used to spark ideas off other people and to develop initially weak ideas, building on a wider range of experience. The technologies are applied slightly differently – electronic mail will normally be sequential, whereas a bulletin board puts the process in front of several or many people at once – but the outcome is similar. A number of techniques lend themselves to this 'contribute and pass it on' approach.

Software to directly support creativity techniques falls into two camps. The most highly developed are packages which are used to structure information. This is particularly important at the early stages of the creative process, when a picture is being gathered of the problem itself and its surroundings. The simplest approach is an outliner, but many programs draw mind maps or similar diagrams for connecting ideas and information. The second group of packages provide direct support to creativity techniques. The advantage of using a computer system rather than working a technique 'by hand' are the prompts that the system gives (sometimes it is difficult to remember techniques) and the ability to record input in a structured way. Most such software is shareware, of mixed quality, but there are increasingly professional products available.

Information technology support is certainly not necessary to implement an innovation programme or to foster individual creativity, but to ignore the contribution IT can make is to push to one side a freely available resource. There are few businesses now where a personal computer is not available, and increasingly few without Internet connection. Information technology is a useful adjunct to most applications of creativity.

Beyond techniques

'True creativity comes from the void. It is only when we surrender and empty our busy minds that we allow space for our creativity potential to be made known.' *Alex Nicholas of Alexander Consulting*

Creativity techniques are a means to an end – releasing the inherent creativity and ability to innovate that we all have to some degree within us. There is some argument for going beyond techniques. In *Hare Brain and Tortoise Mind* (Fourth Estate, 1997), Guy Claxton suggests that there are two approaches to problem-solving and idea generation. We can scurry off towards the solution, hare fashion, or allow the problem to swill around in our brain while the unconscious works on it with tortoise-like patience. From his reviews of cognitive science research, Claxton suggests that by making less conscious effort to think about a problem we can increase our effective intelligence. He suggests we need a new, child-like mode of thinking which is comfortable with ambiguity and uncertainty.

Of itself, this does not preclude the use of creativity techniques. After all, the techniques are all about creating a child-like mode of thinking which is comfortable with ambiguity and uncertainty. When using an effective creativity technique (as opposed to, say, brainstorming), the whole approach depends on putting the problem to one side to let the morass of influences and associations we all carry around with us take charge. Yet some have used Claxton's argument to suggest that modern creativity techniques fall foul of the same problem as brainstorming because however much a creativity technique gives the impression of moving away from the real problem, we are still pushing with hare-like impatience towards a solution. Proponents of this view sometimes argue that we should adopt more of the approach of an Eastern philosophy, prepared to step back from the world in contemplation, without any underlying drivers.

What such an argument misses is the need to cope with both worlds that is mandated by the business pressures of reality. The creativity technique is an ideal mechanism for briefly entering a different way of thinking – in Alex Nicholas's terms surrendering to the void – while retaining an ultimate goal. Creativity without an end-point is not an option for business; arguably it is not creativity at all. Yet while navel-gazing is not the answer, regular use of creativity techniques does seem to develop a sort of Zen creativity – the technique of not having a technique. It is empirically true that regular use of creativity techniques makes it easier to simply 'be creative' without needing to use a technique. However, although this concept has surface similarities to the idea of untargeted meditation, it remains a practical approach with clear targets – it is just that the process has become internalized.

Executive summary

- Effective creativity depends on thinking about a problem in a different way, then avoiding early evaluation before the new idea is fully formed.
- Creativity is best seen as a four-stage process: identifying the question, generating answers, polishing the outcome and implementation.
- Business creativity can be triggered by certain conditions in the business process: when determining strategy, starting a project, devising a new product or service, and where a specific problem occurs.
- Skill in creativity depends on regular practice: building a climate where creativity is encouraged, with regular creativity exercises whether or not there is an immediate problem, will be extremely beneficial.
- Creativity is both a group and an individual process. Individuals are the best sources of initial ideas; groups are the best way to refine and make practical an idea.
- Information technology is increasingly valuable in supporting creativity. Standard office software, bespoke creativity software and the World Wide Web are all important tools. Information technology can support creativity by providing information about the problem and techniques, and by directly implementing a technique.
- With practice it is possible, to some degree, to go beyond techniques. In business terms, however, this is not about total disengagement from reality. Creativity without techniques becomes increasingly easier as techniques are used more, but to have business value creativity must remain focused on specific goals.

Chapter 4

The innovation powerhouses

This chapter begins by looking at the prime sources of information on creativity in the world today. It goes on to examine how companies treat creativity and the ways that they can encourage creativity: by developing a culture that supports it, by using techniques in business processes and by developing a range of creativity resources inside and outside the company.

Today's creativity sources

> 'Look, you've got choices and one of them is to create, be copied but to stay ahead. Your need for creativity is constant. The other choice is to be a sheep.' *Henry Berry, director, Theory B*

Although the original gurus of business creativity are still going strong, de Bono and von Oech have been joined by many other consultants who combine practical business experience with an ability to expound lucidly on the benefits of creativity.

In the USA, the figure of John Kao rides high. Like many of the academics in creativity, Kao has a background in psychology, but he has wide business experience, has lectured at Harvard Business School, and has connections with Stanford and MIT's prestigious Media Lab. Kao likens business creativity to jazz (a personal interest of his). He considers the sort of creativity needed in business to be like jazz improvisation. There is still structure, but the way the music progresses depends on the skills of the players, not the imposed rules of sheet music.

In the UK, four names stand out. Henry Berry's Theory B organization is a grouping of independent consultants who have a like-minded approach to business problem-solving. Particularly focused on facilitating the decision process, Berry's approach is to use theatrical settings to move the participants away from their conventional ways of thinking. Anything from a high-technology science laboratory, to couches and low lighting have been used to provoke a response from participants. Paul Birch and Brian Clegg have developed a significant following by pulling together creativity techniques into a practical framework, rather than leaving it as a grab bag of tools. Their approach combines the 'imagination engineering' framework with a heavy reliance on humour, bringing the lightness of touch of US creativity in the British environment. Professor Tudor Rickards, at Manchester Business School, has managed to develop a theoretical slant on creativity without losing contact with the reality of the business world.

Any overview of the big names in creativity would have to include Synectics. Where most business creativity is a cottage industry, Synectics has made it into a worldwide business. George Prince and Bill Gordon developed the Synectics approach in the early 1960s. Although based on the same basic principles as all creativity techniques, Synectics is the most codified and structured approach, which will appeal particularly to those who like the rigours of systems analysis or other rule-based disciplines. The only danger with this is that the creativity itself becomes inflexible. Synectics has thrived by franchising and training trainers across the world.

Although not working specifically in the field of creativity, it would be careless to overlook the contributions of two general business gurus. Tom Peters's themes can be followed in the titles of his best-selling books, moving from advocating excellence, through thriving on chaos to establishing the need for a crazy organization to deal with crazy times. Peters does not espouse any particular approach to creativity, but is certain of the need for it, labelling innovation and zest as the two prime drivers of differentiation. Many of his case studies are all about the drive for creativity. Charles Handy, the leading British business writer, also espouses innovation, although less explicitly. All Handy's concepts are intensely creative, and require creativity to make them practical, but the creative content in his writing is essentially implicit.

When looking for written inspiration, it is worth adding two other sources which can be very effective in the creativity field. The best business humour combines pointed attack on what's wrong with business and pointers towards a different direction. As humour is a powerful weapon for creativity, these books provide excellent inspiration. Good starting points would be Robert Townsend's *Up the Organization* books (Michael Joseph, 1970), and Scott Adams' masterly *Dilbert* series (Boxtree). A rather different slant comes from the business/biography books which provide a narrative on how a business has succeeded (or failed). Whether watching the rise and rise of Microsoft and Intel or the uncomfortable thrashings of the BBC, such books provide a very useful stimulus for creativity.

Creativity is a field where it is common to claim every idea for your own and ignore the work that has been put in by your predecessors. Inevitably, this survey of the hot sources of creativity as we near the new millennium is biased and limited – apologies to all those who have been unwittingly omitted.

The company experience

'Creativity (or rather innovation) is absolutely critical to my organization and should be for any marketing organization. Our responsibility is to innovate and constantly improve our products. It's in the interests of the consumer. It is also in the interests of the business as creativity can be a significant differentiation when the market is as "noisy" and competitive as the IT industry! For Microsoft to stay ahead, we have to constantly challenge ourselves to "think outside the box", and come up with new ideas that excite the market. It's a way that an organization can reinvent itself and its products in order to deliver value to its customers and to stay ahead of the competition. Life would also be pretty boring if we were not trying to maximize our efforts behind creativity.' *David Svendsen, Managing Director, Microsoft UK*

There are four principle approaches to creativity that will be found in companies large and small around the world. The most popular of all is to ignore it entirely, to regard creativity as the sole property of the advertising agency (and marketing on a good day). This approach makes the assumption that experience and the way we have always done things will allow a company to carry on successfully. Unfortunately, all the trends suggest that this is not a sustainable approach. Companies who apply one of the other three approaches to creativity will be looking at the customers of these type one companies with greedy anticipation.

The second approach is to recognize the importance of creativity, by making sure that your company recruits creative people. This is, of course, easier said than done. The need is to recruit individuals who will be creative in their job, not necessarily creative in an interview (though often there is enough overlap to make this practical). When recruiting an executive, there is more hope, as it is possible to examine his or her track record of creativity. For the rest of the employees there is more risk attached, but it is still well worth trying. Type two companies are bursting with bright young things who are really out to change the world. They will certainly do better than type one companies, but there is a danger that the creativity that is introduced lacks discipline and application.

The third approach is to develop a creative culture in the company. A culture that supports and encourages creativity makes all the difference. It is not enough, though, to put a line in the corporate report and accounts saying 'we support and encourage creativity'. It means rewarding appropriate risk-taking, being prepared to accept failure as a step on the road to success, and all the positive steps that are listed in this book. Only with this third approach does creativity really enter the company. Incidentally, the company types include all earlier approaches, so a type three company may well recruit for creativity as well as having an appropriate culture.

The final step for companies who take creativity seriously is to make use of creativity techniques in the processes of the company. These are companies which have taken on the creative culture and now want to arm their staff with the skills to make creativity a practical everyday tool. Type four companies are few and far between – and so stand an excellent chance of making creativity the factor that will ensure that they can maintain and improve on differentiation and their competitive position.

A culture of creativity

'Organizations depend on people *not* being brave enough to challenge the status quo. They rely for their survival, their continuance on people who are happy, literally, to *continue* what came before. (We derive the word 'continue' from Latin words which mean 'to hold together' whereas Handy's 'discontinuous thinking' would threaten to break things apart.)

This is especially true in time of rapid change: stress makes us want to reproduce the ideas and ways of doing things that we are already used to, and to conform to the behaviours which are exhibited by the majority. Challenging the norms is an even greater stressor. As one manager expressed it to me, in a vivid image that is still seared in my mind's eye: "I'd rather cut my legs off at the knee than risk sticking my head above the parapet."' *David Firth, Consultant*

There are many ways that creativity is being actively supported and encouraged in companies today. They are all valuable. But without one underlying requirement being fulfilled it is unlikely that any will have more than a localized effect. It is generally agreed that without a culture of creativity, a company is unlikely to be able to encourage effective innovation.

The reasoning is simple enough. If it 'feels right' to be creative, to have ideas and to make them known, to challenge conventional thinking, then it will happen. If the employees feel that the inevitable reaction to 'putting their heads above the parapet' is to have them shot off, new ideas will be suppressed, problems will go unsolved and the company will fall into a condition of bureaucratic inertia. As it will clearly be dangerous to come up with their own ideas, frontline staff will be unwilling to take actions without authorization.

Probably the biggest hurdle to overcome in developing a culture for innovation is the need for open communications. Most large companies with hierarchical organizations frown on communication outside the chain of command. Information about the company (or anything else) is filtered down from the top in a carefully controlled manner. For creativity to be natural, this state of affairs has to go out of the window. Anyone in the company should be able to access whatever information is needed to get the job done – here intranets and the Internet (the Net) come into their own (see 'Electronic resources' later in this chapter). Communication between different layers (in both directions) should be a casual matter of routine.

Communication between layers

John Ruscoe, an employee of the UK computer firm ICL, works from a sheep farm in the remote Orkney Islands: 'I have access to everyone in ICL by e-mail. It's considered my right to mail the chief executive if I need to – and to get a reply. That mutual respect is what's needed more than anything else.'

The culture of free communication is a necessary step on the way to the culture of creativity.

The other essential for a culture that supports creativity is tolerance of risk-taking. Many large companies are risk averse. It is not uncommon to be told 'you only get one chance to get it right in this company'. Even the total quality management (TQM) movement (see Chapter 7) can prove a problem in this respect, if the 'get it right first time' message is taken out of production into the workplace in general. Where creativity is desired, risk has to be accepted. The way to encourage creativity is to encourage intelligent risk-taking and failure. This is not intellectual joyriding. It is not advocating taking wild risks for the sake of it, but is advocating being prepared to take a measured risk, accept failure for its learning benefits and get on with more innovation.

Risk-taking at Intel

The organization's attitude to risk is, says Dr Albert Yu, Senior Vice-President and General Manager of the Microprocessor Products Group at Intel Corporation, one of the principle reasons for Intel's success. At Intel, Dr Yu says in his book *Creating the Digital Future* (Free Press, 1998), it is acceptable to fail provided you are taking an informed risk. That may be the route to occasional failure, but it is the only approach that can provide consistent excellence when faced with a fast-changing environment.

Risk-taking at Coca-Cola

Coca-Cola is another company that takes its creativity seriously. It used to be the case that Coca-Cola was regarded as extremely staid. However, senior management at the venerable soft drinks firm now sees creativity as a primary discipline – not a quick hit, but an everyday reality. For Coca-Cola it is essen-

> tial that ideas are treated with respect and given the chance to grow. The
> reasoning behind this is simple – creativity translates directly into competitive
> edge.

It is worth noting that the steps to promote a high-communication, risk-taking,
trusting culture could have a profound effect on the organization. The more
communication, then action, moves away from the traditional hierarchy, the
more likely the company is to take the steps towards a radical shake-up of
the organization – to DisOrganization (see 'Doing it differently' in this
chapter). It is technically possible to develop a culture for creativity without
changing the organization, but it should be realized that once the floodgates
of creativity are opened, everything can and should come under scrutiny,
including the organizational structure.

What about discipline?

'Success comes from taking the path of maximum advantage instead
of the path of least resistance.' *George Bernard Shaw*

Two adjectives which do not fit well together in most people's minds are
'creative' and 'disciplined'. Creativity is all about free flow of ideas and
'letting things all hang out', while discipline is rigid, structured and repeti-
tive. In fact, despite this impression, discipline is essential for effective creativity. Most effective writers apply a significant amount of discipline. They do
not sit around, contemplating infinity and waiting for the muse to strike. They
sit down at the word processor (or pad and pen or dictation machine) and
write. It does not matter what, they write. Sometimes the outcome is rubbish,
but more often than not it is just as creative as waiting for inspiration, with
a much better chance of meeting the deadline.

Deadlines provide a very good measure of effective creativity. Being able
to meet a deadline is a mark of professionalism in creativity – a move away
from amateur tinkering. If business creativity requires implementation to be
truly creative, then meeting a requirement is what it is all about.

However, there is a dangerous trap that awaits those who are attracted by
the siren song of discipline. It is possible to confuse discipline of output with
discipline of input. Provided the creative output is of high quality and delivered on time, it does not depend on how the output is assembled – whether,
for example, the participants turned up for work on time, or wore suits, or
spent half the morning playing Nerf ball in the hall. Creativity can be called
to order over reasonable timescales, looking at desired outputs, but it can just
as easily be hindered by imposing restrictions on the way the ideas are
created. This may seem at odds with the discipline of sitting down to work,
whether or not the muse has struck, but the distinction here is personal. There

cannot be a set time for everyone to be creative, but everyone can set a time for themselves.

To show how dangerous a trap this is, even a high-technology firm like Intel can fall into it. For many years Intel operated an 8 a.m. sign-in. If you arrived more than five minutes after the 8 o'clock deadline you had to sign a book like a naughty schoolchild. Intel also has monthly 'Mr Clean' inspections of everywhere from engineering to marketing to make sure the work areas are nice, clean and tidy. The trouble is, many people work better in clutter, or from mid-afternoon until late into the night. As we will see, creativity is largely an individual activity, while the enhancement and implementation of a creative idea is largely a team activity. To provide the best support for creativity, a company needs to support both – which means allowing plenty of individuality of input, while ensuring great communications and disciplined output.

Yet if a runaway success like Intel can recommend discipline on input as well as output, can it be so wrong? Unfortunately, yes. Intel is highly unusual in having such a narrowly specified product line, combined with massive demand and entrenched backward compatibility. Intel is a true special case. For the rest of us, it is essential to ensure that the discipline we apply to creativity is focused on outputs, not inputs. In the long term Intel, too, will have to learn this lesson if it is to thrive.

Rewarding innovation

'I see this [the need for creativity] mainly in negative terms – people who are not creative (as is widespread in academia, particularly with today's emphasis on "measures of achievement") cannot get out of fixed modes of thinking which make one blind to radically new possibilities.' *Professor Brian Josephson, Cambridge University*

Reward and recognition are key issues in the business of innovation, but they are often given little attention in creativity texts. The assumption seems to be that, given the right techniques, effective innovation will flow naturally into the company. The fact is, though, that most of the potential sources of creativity are not involved in business for some high philosophical pleasure, but for reward. It seems reasonable, then, if creativity is a prime input to the successful business, that we should reward creativity appropriately.

We will see in Chapter 5, in the section 'What is wrong with suggestion schemes?', how the only popular means of explicitly rewarding creativity – the suggestion scheme – is anything but a valuable driver for innovation. If creativity is to become an accepted part of the everyday life of a company it should be explicitly recognized as part of the formal reward package. It may well be that you already reward creativity. Of course you do. When you weigh up what an employee is to be paid, and what non-monetary reward they are to get, you are bound to take their creativity into account. But this is not enough.

If creativity is to be considered important to management, it needs to be brought out of the closet – not just given lip-service in goals and objectives, but reflected in actual payment. Most companies now have some kind of formal assessment scheme. Does your scheme have a particular section on creativity? Look at the example below. How well does this reflect your scheme?

Assessment form, section 2: Creativity
- Takes risks.
- Learns from failure.
- Prepared to put forward apparently silly ideas.
- Produces ten ideas to everyone else's one.
- Builds on the ideas of others, rather than shooting them down.
- Fixes it if it is not broken.
- Knows what the competition is up to, steals it and betters it.

For that matter, if creativity is in your assessment, what priority is it given? If it is true that creativity is an absolute survival skill for most companies, there should be nothing else with higher weighting.

Consider, too, the need to work outside a mechanical annual reward process. How much effort do you put into rewarding specific examples of creativity? Do your managers have the ability to give a substantial reward (ideally a personal present) when someone is particularly creative? Can they issue a reward within days, or even hours? If innovation is to become a central part of the company culture, then rewarding innovation must be as natural as signing an expense claim. Otherwise the message to staff is very clear: 'Creativity is something we really want, but we aren't prepared to pay for it.'

Even when there isn't a concrete reward, it can make a huge difference to ensure that a staff member gets appropriate recognition for creativity. This can range from a pat on the back and congratulations to making sure everyone knows just whose idea it was. Perception pays little attention to speeches and mission statements. Without solid reward and recognition backing it up, there will be little drive for creativity. If, on the other hand, it has clear, quick rewards, if creative actions result in general recognition, innovation will become the everyday component of business life it has to be.

Innovation resources

'Technically we organize regular "brainstorms", a little like (but shorter) than the "think camps" run by the likes of Microsoft, where we try and force the creativity to flow. By concentrating, "thinking" of being creative we find that we usually can be. In fact, sometimes to distraction. Usually these meetings are chaired by the main thinker in our organization – that's me. It's part of my job, and a talent I seem to have, to come up with new ways to write software. I usually start the ball rolling by chucking something out – some "bright idea" that's not clear in my head but that, nevertheless, has been nagging on at me. We find that this "thing", however, might not be the catalyst for innovation. It might come to nothing. However, just by thinking about thinking we're almost certain to be on to something else very quickly.' *Peter J. Morris, Technical Director and Lord of Funk, The Mandebrot Set*

The company that is prepared to take creativity seriously has a wide range of resources available to improve the way individuals and groups within the company can respond creatively to the challenges they face. These resources are examined in more detail in the rest of this chapter. But it must be remembered that without a culture that supports, or even demands creativity, these resources will be little used and will eventually waste away. Such a culture can be started in pockets in a company and, if it is lucky, can succeed in persuading the rest of the company that creativity is essential. But any attempt to grow a climate of creativity without support from the top of the company will eventually founder.

The resources broadly come down to techniques, people, organizational structures and technology. The techniques are given greater coverage in Chapter 3 – for now they are taken for granted. Human resources (as opposed to the HR department) are needed to provide training in these techniques and to give consultancy on the application of creativity and the development of a culture of creativity. People can also provide the resources to facilitate specific creativity sessions to ensure the benefits of techniques are achieved, even if the participants have no personal experience of using them. The organization can help by making creativity part of specific internal processes (see 'Innovation in the business process' in this chapter), and by providing innovation centres and similar facilities. Information technology both enables the free flow of communications – an essential for creativity – and supports the creative process.

Facilitators and consultants

'[Creativity is] seeing what everyone else has seen, but thinking what no one else has thought.' *Brian Lincoln, creativity consultant*

Most companies are currently type one or two in the previous descriptions (see 'The company experience' in this chapter). At best they are intentionally recruiting creative staff; at worst they are riding along with the status quo, seemingly unaware of the brick wall they are heading towards. Without some help, they are unlikely to achieve a change of direction. Once it is accepted that there is a need for enhanced creativity, the company is liable to be in need of assistance.

At the primary level this can come in two forms. If a company is looking to move up to type three or four it will need to develop a culture that fosters creativity. Guidance from consultants is often essential in making this happen. It is too easy when wearing the blinkers of familiarity not to see all the blockages your company puts in the way of creativity.

There may also be an urgent need to attack specific problems and requirements for ideas. Here it is valuable to bring in a consultant to facilitate creativity sessions, providing expertise in the techniques and approaches of creativity combined with a detachment from the problem. A good facilitator can make all the difference to a creativity session, helping the participants both in the execution of the techniques and in teasing the great ideas from the output.

Training

'A Sufi tale:
"Who guided you in the Way?"
"A dog. One day I saw him by the riverside almost dying of thirst. Each time that he looked to the water, the water reflected his image, he was scared and withdrawing as he thought there was another dog. Finally he was so desperate, his need was so big, that he jumped into the water, and as he jumped the other dog faded away. The dog discovered that the obstacle was himself. The barrier between him and what he wanted disappeared."' *José Ferrandis, Marketing Management Consultant, Ferrandis and Partners (Madrid)*

Even more than consultancy, training is a valuable long-term resource. While it may always prove useful to bring in consultants to facilitate major decision-making sessions, or groups of individuals who have not time to be trained in creativity, the majority of the staff will benefit hugely from such training. Training reinforces the message that the company takes creativity seriously, stresses how much creativity should be part of everyday business and gives staff experience of using techniques.

Exactly how much training will be required depends on circumstances. A brief introduction (perhaps two hours) as part of a broader training programme will be enough to give a flavour of what creativity is about. A one-day session will give the participant practical experience of using techniques and a feel for when and how to bring them into play. Typically two to three days will be required to train those individuals who are expected not only to manage their own creativity, but to facilitate creativity in others. When measured against the potential benefits, this is a small investment.

The corporate jester

'Creativity means never having to say you're sorry.' *Paul Birch, ex Corporate Jester, British Airways*

The corporate jester is a very special form of creativity consultant.

British Airways

In 1995 British Airways hit the headlines, not for reasons of business triumph or industrial unrest, but because of a job title. The then chief executive, Sir Colin Marshall, had authorized a new position in the company – Corporate Jester. In interviews at the time, the Jester himself, Paul Birch was quoted as saying 'A big company is a bit like a medieval court, where the king can do no wrong. No one questions the king or the senior courtiers. But if you're not careful, this can lead you down the abyss.' The post of Corporate Jester was inspired by an article in *New Management* (vol. 2, no. 2, 1984) by D. Verne Morland – 'Lear's Fool: Coping with Change Beyond Future Shock'. Birch's conception was of an experienced manager who was prepared to take risks (more than one newspaper article at the time pointed out that the jester might lose his head if the king (or possibly Lord King) lost his sense of humour). In essence, the role was to stick his nose into senior management business and comment constructively.

This is an approach that will not work everywhere. A Confederation of British Industry (CBI) spokeswoman was quoted at the time as saying: 'It's very new and none of the committees have had a chance to discuss it yet.' Birch lasted about eighteen months in the role, before a reorganization placed him elsewhere. There is no doubt though that, with the right person in the job, this is a very powerful option for the innovation agenda. The strength of a medieval jester was being able to say things others would not dare from a position of (relative) safety – an ideal standpoint for bringing creativity into a company. A corporate jester can only succeed with complete support from the top of the company, but given that remit there is an unrivalled opportunity to point out the stupidities and opportunities for creativity which otherwise are usually ignored because it is not acceptable to criticize the people at the top. Many companies would benefit from a period of having a corporate jester, even if few may ever take on the challenge.

Innovation centres and other organizational fillips

There are a number of ways an organization can provide support to the creative process. Some companies have tried setting up a creativity centre. Such an approach is usually relatively short-lived. Centres of this kind are prime targets whenever cost-cutting is in vogue, and there is some doubt as to the message they put across. If the centre is there merely as a catalyst to point to and provide resources, the approach is fine, but often it is seen as the place that 'does' creativity, which has a detrimental effect on the spread of the creativity culture through the company. After all, there is no need for everyone to be creative if a there is a centre to do it for you.

What certainly is valuable is providing access to books, training and other indirect resources. This is unlikely to require a dedicated centre, but typically will fit within a company's management training scope. However, larger companies may well feel justified in having an innovation manager – someone responsible for bringing innovation in and out of the company to the attention of the company as a whole. The innovation manager will typically have few if any staff, but should be an excellent communicator. As well as making the successes (and, equally important, the failures) of innovation widely known through the company, the innovation manager should also be responsible for broadening an understanding of what creativity is, how it functions and the benefits of using creativity techniques.

Probably the most useful organizational inputs to creativity, however, come from the subculture. Groups of individuals with a part-time interest in creativity can make a big difference to the way a company acts by bringing creativity into their everyday roles. Some companies have lunchtime creativity groups which meet informally to practise creativity techniques and offer free consultancy to other parts of the company. In a typical session of this sort, a problem-owner will bring a problem to the group, which will then use two or three techniques to explore the problem and generate ideas. The problem-owner can then go away with a whole collection of relevant and innovative ideas, all out of a simple lunchtime session. If such creativity groups form (or are seeded) in a company, it is worth considering funding lunches for them – not a bad return for the typical output.

Electronic resources

'We have a series of "closed" (meaning that they're not publicly available) Microsoft Exchange discussion groups running on our main mail server here. These too allow people to discuss ideas. It's this discussion, talking about "things" that's so important. The ability to bounce ideas off of like-minded peers that makes innovation and that's why we're so careful about who we employ.' *Peter J. Morris, Technical Director and Lord of Funk, The Mandebrot Set*

Used correctly, the new tools of electronic communication are proving an essential aid to creative development. They are not enough on their own. Without the right culture, innovation cannot thrive. Without appropriate techniques and training, creativity will be limited to the accidental and serendipitous. Without the right people, there will not be the individuality and extra pizzazz to go beyond the everyday. And without regular face-to-face contact, electronic communication is simply not enough. But electronic tools are second only to basic creativity techniques in enhancing the potential for creativity, and particularly for building on and developing an initial creative idea. The main electronic resources involved are electronic mail (e-mail), Notes and bulletin boards, intranets, the World Wide Web and specific creativity tools (see Figure 4.1).

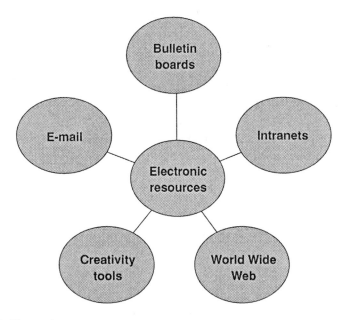

Figure 4.1 Electronic resources

E-mail is now becoming ubiquitous. At first sight, while an excellent way of communicating, it is no more relevant to creativity than the traditional post office mail. However, the immediacy of e-mail makes it a totally different communication medium. That immediacy results in two major differences. First, fewer ideas are lost. Ideas have a tendency to pop up when it is not practical to deal with them. No one would think of sitting down to write a letter to someone who could do something with that idea. The immediacy of e-mail means that it is possible to send off an e-mail to the most appropriate person to deal with the idea, rather than leaving it to fester. The process is so quick that it can be performed as the idea occurs, in the middle of other work, rather than put to one side and forgotten.

The second impact of e-mail is in bringing in a much bigger resource pool than was previously available. Provided the e-mail creativity resource is nurtured by ensuring that staff build their electronic contacts databases assiduously, a whole new source of creative input is available whenever it needs to be called on. What is more, the way a single e-mail message can be sent out to many recipients also gives greater leverage.

The light sabre incident

At a meeting, a client divulged as an entertainment that he thought he had a theoretical basis for the workings of a Star Wars style light sabre. This would be a powerful beam of light that extended a fixed distance, then stopped. Curious, I sent the idea to a physicist contact, who came back with a whole range of thoughts on the matter. Part of the response is reproduced below in case the example has whetted your curiosity, but the lesson is more important. E-mail contacts around the world can be a superb resource for innovation, as it takes so much less effort to respond to an e-mail than any other communication, so it is much more practical to elicit a response.

The spatial variation of the beam you describe is equivalent to a box car function (i.e. it starts and stops, stays constant in the middle, but otherwise does not go anywhere else). So its (spatial) frequency content is just the Fourier transform of the box car – i.e. a sinc function (basically $\sin k / k$, where k is proportional to spatial frequency $= c / L$). Thus, the beam you describe could be built up from a light source with the corresponding spectrum, although I don't know how you could construct a spectrum to order like it. For one thing, it would need infinite bandwidth to stop at a precise point. However, assuming you don't mind the beam tailing off a little (in particular, consistent with the uncertainty principle), it might be possible ... except that that only solves half the problem (the easy half!). The big problem would be getting the phase of the frequencies right (remember that, in general, Fourier transforms require complex amplitudes). This is because the phase of the transform is zero (in this case, if you choose a convenient origin at the centre of the beam, the amplitudes are purely real), which means that it cannot be built using a source of illumination from one side only. In fact, you need a symmetric source in space, hence ... one possibility might be to use two beams of light travelling in opposite directions. This can easily be done using a mirror, but I guess that would be cheating (of course, two mirrors with a light source in the middle would clinch it, and the light would no longer need to be coherent!).

In any case, without mirrors, the beams would have to interfere constructively over the required distance, and destructively elsewhere. Again, I am not sure how you would do it, but ... of course, in a quantum world almost anything goes. Certainly there are some strange effects with (entangled states of) light beams/particles where you might be able to infer that a beam stopped at a particular location because of something you did somewhere else (e.g. in the case of Schrodinger's cat or the Stern-

Gerlach experiment), but you could not actually say that the light/particle existed between the points where it started and where you said it ended (indeed, technically, until the moment of observation, it was everywhere between and beyond the point you are interested in). Interestingly, these types of effects can be observed routinely in the laboratory and have recently even been used to teleport an object (actually an ion) from one side of a laboratory to another (I kid you not!). But that is relatively easy, and you did say that you wanted a light sabre and not a teleporter! (Also, I can do time travel for you, but I am sure you know how to do that anyway.)
Dr Helmut Jakubowicz

As already discussed in Chapter 3, bulletin boards, particularly the powerful Lotus Notes product, provide a mechanism for taking the idea sharing of e-mail into a parallel processing world that makes it easier to share both problems and solutions. Intranets are a special case of the same phenomenon. An intranet is a mini-World Wide Web, existing only on the computers of a particular company. It has all the friendliness and ease of use of the Web, providing fast access to a wide range of company information. It can also be made very easy for individuals to contribute information to an intranet. Levi Strauss & Co., for example, sets great store by its intranet, Eureka, which is used both to distribute corporate information and as a way for the employees to contribute to an ongoing discussion. The advantage of an intranet over bulletin boards or Notes is the particularly visual presentation – always a plus for creativity – and the simplicity of the environment compared with a heavyweight like Notes. The intranet is also capable of linking transparently to the wider World Wide Web, so the whole Web is available as a resource to back up items on the intranet.

The World Wide Web is a strange facility. Since access to appropriate information is essential to the first part of the creative process – understanding the problem area and potential solution space – the Web's unique ability to provide information on almost anything is unparalleled in history. On top of this, as mentioned in Chapter 3, the Web can be used as a creative stimulation tool in its own right. This being the case, it is very sad that almost all the reports that are published about wide access to the Web focus on misuse – working time wasted and pornography downloaded. Such reports are distinctly naïve. They assume that, were it not for Web access, the staff involved would spend their whole time in productive work. In fact, any knowledge work (which tends to be the areas where Web access is widely available) is sporadic, interlaced with sometimes lengthy non-productive periods. The more creative the individual, the more likely there is to be contrast between high productivity and non-productive times. All our understanding of creativity suggests that such time would be valuably spent surfing the Net, picking up a huge range of influences and possible new directions. Anti-social use of the Web needs to be acknowledged as unacceptable, but beyond that, to put controls on Web access is to deny the sort of trust that engenders creativity.

Electronic traps

Much has been made of the dangers of wasting time surfing the Internet instead of working. A more insidious danger with the use of electronic communications is the devaluation of conventional face-to-face contact. Yet it is casual, social contact which generates many of the best ideas. When Oticon Chief Executive Lars Kolind began his transformation of the company, he banned e-mail in the early stages. Yet e-mail is a crucial tool to bringing creativity to a large company, as discussed above.

The trick of avoiding the electronic trap is to keep e-mail in its place. It should not be seen as an alternative to chatting with anyone in close proximity. A workgroup should not be using e-mail (or Notes) as its primary means of communication – face-to-face communication is the only way to ensure creative interaction. And that goes for any workgroup, whether it is a small, localized unit, a cross-functional project team or the board. There needs to be plenty of opportunity for regular, face-to-face interaction. But e-mail should be used, much more than it is at present, as a way of bringing the wider community in to support the workgroup, whether it is other parts of the same organization or external contacts. It is interesting that many large companies still have restrictions on e-mail external to the company while having free access to internal e-mail. Arguably, they have this picture upside down.

Finally, we come to the specific creativity tools. Software has been written to cover many aspects of creativity, but as suggested in Chapter 3, the two prime business product areas are idea-mapping – supporting the production of mind maps and similar diagrams – and technique support. At the moment, such software is regarded as niche. If it is bought at all, it is either by enthusiasts, using their own credit cards, or by specialist areas of the company such as operational research, which regard problem-solving to be part of their specific remit, and are used to buying non-standard, specialist software. If creativity is to become as much a part of a company's processes as finance, creativity software should become no more remarkable than a spreadsheet.

Innovation in the business process

'When I have won a victory I do not repeat my tactics, but rearrange them in an infinite variety of ways to meet the circumstances.' *Sun Tzu, The Art of War*

In Chapter 3 we looked at the 'when' of fitting creativity into the business process:

- When determining strategy.
- When starting a project.

- When devising a new product or service.
- When a specific problem occurs.
- When regularly practising creativity techniques for self-development.

Now we can consider the what and how of making innovation an integral part of the process. There are two principle activities which should be incorporated into the business process. Whether or not the intention is to make use of creativity techniques to generate ideas and solve problems, it is worth using the first-stage techniques to ensure that the right topic is being covered. Here the aim is to ensure that the background is adequately covered, and that the goal is a valid one. See Chapter 2 for more information.

The biggest contribution of creativity, however, comes in developing new ideas and problem solutions. If there is a formal process for developing strategy, or authorizing projects, it makes sense to ensure that undertaking a creativity session is part of the checklist. This need not be a major exercise – it could be all over in fifteen minutes, but the crucial requirement is to use one or more creativity techniques to explore possible solutions. See Chapter 2 for more on the techniques themselves.

In the early stages of introducing creativity to a company, these techniques may seem alien. Some groups, particularly the more senior, may never undertake the training necessary to use the techniques. When a high-level group needs to come up with a creative solution, it is often sensible to involve an external facilitator to ensure that the full strength of the creativity technique is brought to bear. For many other occasions, as expertise in creativity within the company grows, it should be enough to have those involved in the decision-making use a technique directly.

Because any technique can become stale with overuse, it is important not to write a specific technique into the company's processes. After all, creativity is about flexibility, and it is just getting into a different rut to prescribe a particular approach. Instead, a tool bag of techniques should be available to call on at the appropriate point. There is an opportunity with the spread of intranets and Lotus Notes to have technique summaries available in electronic form and call them up when needed.

As a company takes on the innovation culture, it will seem more and more natural to use a technique as part of a meeting discussing a problem, just as more traditional techniques like SWOT (strengths, weaknesses, opportunities and threats) analysis might be brought into play. However, it is important to follow through with the later processes of selection and evaluation, otherwise the ideas session becomes a mild amusement in the line of business, rather than a serious tool for generating an innovative approach.

Making creativity part of the processes is difficult, because the creative approach naturally militates against rules and procedures. It is usually enough to make sure that an appropriate tool bag of techniques is available, that staff have been trained or have an expert facilitator and that the company procedures expect staff to be creative (after all, they will be rewarded on their creativity) and to make use of creativity techniques in key processes such as those listed above.

Hiring for innovation

> '"Creative people" are those who aren't taken seriously by their fellow travellers – first time round. Creativity is invariably that which others have but no one can recognize in themselves; it is always elusive if you look for it but can surprise when least expected.' *Ian Campbell, Financial Services Manager*

As the central understanding of business creativity is that anyone's creativity can be enhanced using creativity techniques, it might seem strange that a contributor to the potential for innovation is hiring the right people. Actually, there is no conflict. The fact that anyone's creativity can be dramatically enhanced does not deny that some people are more creative than others are. Consciously or unconsciously, when recruiting, we are deciding to encourage or discourage creative people from joining the organization. More often than not, we discourage.

This is not a simple picture. To handle the complexities and challenges of the modern business world, it would be ideal if everyone could have enhanced creativity, whether they are the cleaner or the chief executive. A cleaner who can spot a customer wandering lost around the store and do something about it rather than ignore them because it is not his or her job is an asset. A chief executive who has the creativity to see beyond what has always been done is an essential for survival. Yet this does not mean we want to recruit the most creative people into all posts. The cleaner and the chief executive both need to be more creative within their boundaries, but neither of these jobs can be filled by someone who is too creative in approach.

In many other roles, the best way to obtain innovation will be to recruit creative people. There are, however, problems attached to this strategy. Creative people require a very different style of management. They need to be managed by respect rather than authority. Since studies by French and Raven in the 1950s, there has been a reasonably clear understanding of the mechanisms of power. The traditional power of management depended on three of French and Raven's classes: reward, coercion and legitimate power – the power awarded by status. Although few will ignore reward, coercion and legitimate power tend to be treated scornfully by creative people. Instead, they are influenced by French and Raven's other two classes: refer- ent power, the power of charismatic leadership, and expert power. However, if this need for a different management style is understood and undertaken, creative people can be hugely productive and provide the essential impetus of innovation. Having creative people in the organization will not remove the need for systematic creativity, but they will provide a huge extra boost.

Do we need them?

If creative people do not remove the need for systematic creativity, does systematic creativity remove the need for really creative people? Not at all. Highly creative individuals will deliver on a totally different scale, in a totally different way to your expectations. They are always worth the effort, if you are capable of putting in the effort.

One of the best-known examples of practical creativity is worth retelling in this context. Art Fry, a scientist at 3M sang in a church choir. He wanted to mark his place in his hymnbook, but the paper kept falling out. He knew that a colleague, Spence Silver, had produced a glue that was a failure. It came unstuck too easily. Fry made the imaginative leap and used Silver's glue to stick paper markers into his hymnbook that could be removed without damaging the book. This inspired the idea of a product – but 3M could not see any demand; the customers were not asking for it. Fry and Silver were reduced to making up a batch of Post-its and walking them round senior executives' secretaries at 3M. Once they were using them and the supply dried up, all of a sudden the powers that be at 3M knew there really was a demand and did something about it.

Fry and Silver's actions took place not within a stifling company, but one of the most creative in existence, where systematic innovation has been a way of life for a long, long time. This atmosphere may well have been responsible for Fry's knowledge of Silver's failed adhesive. Yet to get the Post-it note to market required more – Fry and Silver's personal creativity which took them the extra yard, and gave them the tenacity to fight the system in a positive, innovative way. The Post-it note shows just how much we still need individuals with that special creative edge.

If creative people are difficult to manage, they are also difficult to recruit. Creative people may not have the 'appropriate' qualifications for the job – experience is likely to count much more with them. Creative people will often have much less interest in your company than is generally looked for in a recruit. They will be interested in what they can do as a result of being in the company, not in the company itself. It is to some extent a stereotype, but it remains true that creative people are also less worried about conforming. If you consider a dress code important, if good time-keeping is considered more valuable than outstanding work, you are unlikely to recruit (and certainly will not keep) creative people. Creative people want to work where, when and how they like. In return for putting up with this burden, the company can expect a whole order of magnitude: better output, better ideas, better implementation. If that is not the return, you have got a freeloader, but if it is, creativity was worth fighting for.

Leadership versus management

'There is an important message for leaders everywhere and that is to think about your children. When a child has a crazy idea you encourage and nurture it, knowing that the play will go some way to develop the person and the idea may be useful. One of the sad things about adulthood is that play rarely gets sanctioned, but it's one of the most useful things you can do.' *Henry Berry, director, Theory B*

Whether dealing with the classic creative person described in the previous section, or merely running a company that has creativity at the heart of its operation, there needs to be a different approach to management. Traditional management is about setting a series of specific objectives. As the employee meets these, they are ticked off. At the end of the year, they can be neatly assessed. Neat is the key word. Management by objectives is easy to do, but it does not deliver the flexibility that is needed to adapt and react to a fast-changing competitive world. What is needed instead is leadership.

Unlike the manager's clearly defined objectives, the leader communicates principles. These do not tell the employee what to do, but set the framework within which the employee can decide on the most appropriate action. Leaders are not as hands on as managers – they are more prepared to let the staff get on with the job, while constantly working on communicating and supporting to ensure that the principles are clear, and that new circumstances from the customer interface get fed back into the principles.

Syrett and Lammiman in *Managing 'Live' Innovation* (Butterworth-Heine-mann, 1998) make the distinction between the solo leader and the team leader. The solo leader is the traditional high-energy boss. He or she plays an unlimited role, wants conformity from their staff, has a tendency to accumulate yes men or women and above all directs. The team leader makes a positive choice to limit his or her own role, brings out and develops colleagues, is always on the lookout for talent and builds on diversity. This picture fits well with John Kao's concept that the manager of creative staff has to be an impresario – someone with plenty of personal drive, who can pick the right people but who is then prepared to leave the limelight to the stars. The 'solo leader' is actually a manager with charisma. The true leader is quite a different proposition. Managers can turn companies around, but they cannot generally follow through; leaders can deal with both challenges.

In *DisOrganization* (FT Pitman Publishing, 1998), Clegg and Birch typify leadership as being about people and about making unreasonable requests. It is about people, because leadership requires trust – a very different approach to the time and task focus of management – and it is about unreasonable requests because leadership expects much more of its employees than management. Management expects the worst and gets it; leadership is quite the reverse. Both sets of authors agree on the fundamental relevance to creativity. Traditional management discourages creativity, leadership nurtures it – it is as simple as that.

Doing it differently

'To innovate is not to reform.' *Edmund Burke, eighteenth-century politician*

As we have seen, there are a number of ways to ensure that creativity becomes embedded in the culture of a company, making it an essential part of the way an organization operates. Yet there is a further level at which some more advanced companies are introducing innovation – being creative about the organization itself. The need for this has been recognized beyond the creativity community. Take the views of top US and UK business gurus, Tom Peters and Charles Handy (Chapter 10, identifies the appropriate books to expand on their views).

Peters has long considered the need for overhaul of the organization to enable it to be differentiated from the competition. After encouraging us to search for excellence and thrive on chaos, his message is now stark. Change is not enough; it is too incremental. The basis for the truly innovative organization is revolution and abandonment. Forget structure and organization charts, Peters's new model for the enterprise is the Rolodex. In essence, Peters argues that we must move from faceless corporate structures to networks of interacting individuals. With such a radical view, the company (organized in small, autonomous groups) takes on the feel and flexibility of the small company, with all its potential for great customer service. It is only with such an approach, Peters argues, that we can move beyond quality to wow!

Handy might have more British restraint, but his message is still one of the importance of the individual. His metaphor for both the individual and the organization is the ring doughnut. In the centre is the hole, the core, the things that have to be done to survive. Handy points out that for the individual, what makes life interesting is usually the surrounding ring – the 'everything else' that makes the difference between survival and worthwhile living. This has come to have more and more significance. He sees organizations moving to a doughnut structure. The directly employed, small essential core will be there, but the difference, the uniqueness of the organization, will come from the way it interacts with its surrounding ring of associates – contract workers and independent professionals, business suppliers and partners.

The clearest picture of taking the plunge with such creative organizational reform comes in Clegg and Birch's *DisOrganization*. This argues for the need to dismiss wishy-washy compromise and embrace both ends of the organizational extremes. By using both management and leadership, by combining reaction with innovation and by grouping totally fragmented mini-companies of no greater than fifty people with a steering netcompany, DisOrganization proposes a radical change in the way companies are run. The weapons provided for this change are clarity and direction, fun and empowerment, and creativity and innovation. These are driven through inward (people, teams, resources and organization) and external (products and services, customers, partners, competitors and communications) channels to achieve the desired change.

The ABB of DisOrganization

Because it is one of the few examples of a large company that has already taken the plunge, the Swedish engineering giant ABB is the favourite case study of all the creative organization experts. Just as an organization can be held back from the necessary major change by the people at the top, Percy Barnevik, the top man at Asea Brown Boveri has pushed his company into a phenomenal transformation. The 200 000 strong business has only 150 people at the centre – the netcompany in Clegg and Birch terminology – while the rest is split into 5000 effectively autonomous units (mini-companies). This was the only way Barnevik could see to incorporate the small company values of speed, flexibility, innovation and superb customer service into a corporate structure. He took a huge gamble, but it has paid off handsomely.

In fact, all of these writers on creative organizational change show the way forward to be both an innovative organization and an organization for innovation. Not only are these innovations as to how an organization works, they are specifically designed to improve the creative input that organization can produce. Key to this are:

- **Communications** – using personal and company networks to assist with problem-solving and feed into idea generation.
- **Lack of hierarchy** – many ideas are frustrated by the hierarchy. In the new picture of organization put forward by the gurus, hierarchy is taken out of the picture, leaving a small company culture where anyone and everyone feels it not only possible but essential to make suggestions for making things better.
- **Focus on the individual** – creativity is initially an individual activity. Without the ability to act as an individual, innovation is unlikely to thrive.
- **Focus on the team** – idea development is best as a team activity. The better the team spirit, the more likely a group will pull together to ensure that an idea is effectively carried through.
- **Acceptance of fun** – creativity thrives in an atmosphere of fun. The traditional, po-faced approach to business dampens down creativity. The gurus emphasize the need for work to be more than a way of earning money; to get the innovative edge it has to be desirable in its own right.

Few companies are yet to go the whole hog and accept the creative organization. It is a concept which is still emerging. Although in principle any company could change the way it works so radically, it is only possible when entirely supported from the top. Many organizations will continue to be held back as long as the top team is holding on to an old-fashioned concept of central control. Without giving up a considerable part of this traditional power it is impossible to achieve the flexible, small-unit approach. This does not mean that such change will not happen. It is already beginning. Natural selection will ensure that the approach spreads. But like all Darwinian processes it will take time.

Creative hearing

Danish hearing-aid manufacturer Oticon was totally restructured in the 1990s. Faced with the introduction of Siemens, the German electronics giant, into its market, Oticon had to change to survive. The company's production was split up into units of thirty to fifty, each divided into workgroups of less than ten. In such a small group, everyone can sensibly know what everyone else is doing. Communication is transformed, buy-in becomes the norm, creativity is part of everyday life. The company has a network organization rather than the traditional hierarchy. Within two years, productivity was up, costs reduced and new products were developed at an unheard of rate.

Like ABB, Oticon's transformation was down to the vision of a charismatic leader – in this case, Chief Executive, Lars Kolind. Without total support from the top of the organization, a change as dramatic as DisOrganization is not possible. Yet without such a change, the full potential for creativity will not be realized. It is interesting that two of the first examples of DisOrganization in action come from Scandinavian companies. It is possible that the traditional Scandinavian disregard for formal hierarchy could make such a change easier to accept than in other, more conservative cultures.

Building for innovation

'In the modern business world, it is not possible to survive without creativity. One day all businesses will know this.' *Julian Patterson, Editor, VNU New Media*

Whether or not the company is radically reorganized, the physical environment of the company can have a significant impact on creativity. The two key trends in changing the environment which can affect innovation are teleworking and the new approach to shared space. It is strange that two such diverse approaches can each enhance innovation. One implies less physical interaction, the other more. One involves fragmenting, the other centralizing. Yet, as the possibilities of organizational creativity have shown, it is often the combination of contrasting extremes that can best handle a creative demand. In fact the two are complementary. Teleworking functions best when combined with the opportunity to make use of good shared space when required.

Teleworking is an odd concept to come under a heading of building for innovation, in that it is almost the reverse of building in the conventional sense. However, when taken under the broad view of where work takes place, teleworking is just another approach to providing a workplace. In many ways teleworking was an idea ahead of its time. When it first began, the technology to support it was limited and the trials made of it half-hearted. The result was often failure, but this was due to weaknesses in the implementation, not the concept.

The general pros and cons of teleworking are well known by now. The employee gets a chance to work in an environment of their choice, often to their own timing. Traffic congestion and time-wasting is disposed of. Flexibility is the name of the game. For some this is a disadvantage. They may not have the right space in which to work at home, or a handy satellite office to work from. They may not want to take charge of their own work to this extent. From the employer's point of view, despite clear demonstrations of reduced costs and improved efficiency, the big problem with teleworking has always been trust. The employer does not trust the employee not to spend all their time on things other than work. This lack of trust is symptomatic of the problems of large organizations, and is unlikely to be wholly removed until a company moves to a more creative organizational structure, which cannot function without trust. In practice, moving to a more task-oriented, less time-driven approach can reduce the need for trust. For a long time, our production-line business mentality has been too controlled by inputs – when does the employee turn up, how long are they sitting at the desk – rather than outputs – what do they actually produce. To make teleworking effective it is best to have an attitude that says it does not matter how or during what hours the employee produces the right output, just that the output is up to quality and on time.

Teleworking has significant advantages for creativity. As has already been described, most original ideas are individual work. More than that, they are usually thought up in convivial surroundings. Teleworking enables employees to work in a space they are comfortable with, dressed how they like, away from many of the distractions and mundane dross of the office. Some teleworkers have experienced huge increases in productivity of brain work when working away from the office, whether in the home, a satellite office, or with a laptop on the beach or in a field.

Yet on its own teleworking is not enough. There is a need to share ideas, to combine them and refine them, if creativity is to be truly enhanced. Some of this can be done by remote communication. E-mail, bulletin boards, the World Wide Web, intranets and extranets (areas of the World Wide Web exclusively for a company and its customers/partners), desktop video-conferencing, can all help collaborative working. But there comes a point where face-to-face communication is the only effective means. Where teleworkers are involved, this might mean meeting off the main company site. Once teleworking seems natural, it seems equally natural to meet in the dining-room of a house, in a pub or in a field – and any of these places are likely to produce more relaxed, effective creative work than in a stuffy office. But often teleworkers will not be involved and there is a need to enhance the shared space in the workplace.

Shared space is a concept which has not long been given much consideration when designing offices and other workplaces. It is the antithesis of the office cubicle, the environment so mocked by Scott Adams, the superb cartoonist who concentrates his irony on the high-technology workplace. Shared space is about recognizing the need for informal meeting and discussion. Almost universally this is acknowledged as the way all the real decisions get made. This suspicion is backed up by research at MIT, which found that about 80 per cent of key implemented ideas arose out of casual chats at the coffee machine and other everyday, non-specific meetings. Yet in many office blocks, the only shared spaces are the canteens and the toilets.

If a building is to be designed to enhance creativity, there needs to be much more opportunity for the fortunate accident. Staff from different parts of the company should routinely be able to bump into each other, to stop for five minutes in pleasant surroundings and make use of formal and informal networks to build on ideas and develop solutions. This calls for a lot more open space – in the UK, ideally under glass – and places to sit outside of the formal structure of an office. The requirement is challenging, but not impossible.

Waterside: the British Airways experience
British Airways took a bold step when establishing its new headquarters building at Harmondsworth, north of Heathrow Airport. Rather than build just another office complex, it was designed from the floor up to enhance the potential for innovation. Central to this is the phenomenal shared space, The Street.

It is widely accepted that most creative ideas generation and effective networking takes part outside of the conventional office. The Street is a glass-covered boulevard with coffee shops and meeting spots. All the office accommodation runs off it – all the life of the building runs through it. As a result, there are many more chance meetings, quick chats, conversations over a coffee than in a normal environment. At the same time, all the office space is as open as possible. Even directors sit in open plan, though there are plenty of meeting rooms for when privacy is required. Those who do not need a fixed location hot-desk with laptop computers. Everyone uses a Lotus Notes e-mail and bulletin board system to share information.

Waterside began occupation in early 1998. After six months, despite the inevitable teething troubles, it was obvious that there were some huge successes. People felt more positive about going in to work. The Street really did generate those essential casual meetings at a phenomenal rate. The open plan did make people seem much more accessible. Hot-desking, perhaps was less of a success – but where the other features were designed to improve interaction, this was more of a practical step to get more people into a limited space. In a mere six months, Waterside had proved that the right approach to space can have a very positive effect on networking and creativity.

Designing space and buildings for innovation is not limited to the white-collar office world. As Syrett and Lammiman point out in *Managing 'Live' Innovation*, German car manufacturer BMW has put together a remarkable structure called FIZ (Forschung Ingenieur Zentrum) which has revolutionized the design and development of new cars, a real mix of office and shop-floor environment. FIZ dates back to the early 1990s, and has had time to prove the considerable benefits (a halved development time, enhanced methods and products) that arose from the investment in appropriate buildings and use of the space.

Although it is possible to achieve some of these advantages of physical change without changing the organization, the best results will come out of a combination of the physical and the organizational. It is rare that teleworking is taken to full advantage in a typical corporate hierarchy because the elements of trust and personal responsibility, essential to make teleworking effective, are not there. If employees move to the small company environment of a doughnut company, a DisOrganized company, a Crazy organization, they have a much more direct link between their actions and their reward. Teleworking becomes a more practical and natural mechanism. Similarly, the shared space concept is an ideal accompaniment to the new company style. In a mini-company everyone can know everyone – the shared space makes this particularly effective, and provides the environment for networking between mini-companies.

With exceptions like British Airways and BMW, very few companies have really thought through the benefits of getting their working space right. To ignore this opportunity to create an environment that encourages universal creativity is remarkably short-sighted.

Executive summary

- Companies' approaches to creativity range from ignoring it to making it part of their day-to-day processes.
- A prime requirement to innovate is a culture of creativity that provides free communication and information, makes it acceptable to take risks (and fail), and makes innovation something that is explicitly rewarded.
- Discipline is important for creativity, but it needs to be discipline of output (deadlines, quality, content, etc.) rather than discipline of input (start times, dress codes etc.).

- Key resources (apart from the techniques themselves) include facilitation and consultancy, training, appropriate buildings, electronic tools and communication facilities.
- It is possible to hire for creativity, but it is not enough.
- Innovation requires leadership rather than management.
- Although it is possible to innovate without significant changes to the organizational structure, building a creative culture is liable to call the current structure into question and point towards a collection of small groups, working autonomously but with superb communications to keep the organization together.

Chapter 5

Swamps and alligators

From the line management viewpoint, it is very easy to see creativity as another fad being imposed from the top to cover up incompetent management. It is essential, however, to get across the practical value of this discipline. Creativity is the classic example of a Pygmalion technology. Unless the user really believes in it, it will not work: perception is extremely important. New ideas are like green shoots; they can be destroyed very easily if they are trampled on by cynicism. This section looks at how those who are up to their necks in alligators may regard the introduction of systematic creativity, and how to sell it to them.

The line manager's story

'New opinions are always suspected and usually opposed, without any other reason but because they are not already common.' *John Locke, seventeenth-century philosopher*

This story concerns a real manager in a real business — but the names have been changed to protect the innocent. Mona was the Operations Manager in charge of running the Data Centre of a large UK manufacturer. As part of a management training exercise which the Chief Executive decreed every manager in the company would go through, Mona and her team spent an afternoon at a management training centre, being introduced to the use of business creativity.

'I've seen it happen before, and no doubt I'll see it again. The top people, with the best intentions in the world, decide that all managers have to have this airy-fairy training. The trouble is, it's fine for marketing people, or even most of the line managers, because they're detached from the real world. My team and I have a very specific commitment – keeping this Data Centre afloat. My staff all know exactly what is expected of them, and have a set of performance measures that make it very plain whether or not they are succeeding. We need the latest American fad, and we need my whole team pulled out like we need holes in our head. It's bad enough having to deal with users, without this as well.

'Even if we did need help, which we don't, surely they could come up with something better than this. We start by playing silly games. Then, when we're trying to solve a serious business problem, they keep expecting us to come up with associations for a picture or ask how an Ancient Egyptian would deal with my problem. It's simply a waste of time. We'll all go back to the office afterwards, do nothing about it and get on with the job, like we should have been in the first place. In the end, all we get out of the training is a break from the phones and a good lunch.'

Mona's picture of creativity (or any other 'trendy' management training) is based on a hugely distorted caricature of the real world. The problem is that her perceptions are very real to her – and to a huge swathe of current management. They are especially common among older managers and those whose jobs are really more supervisory than true management. We will be looking at some of Mona's distortions in more detail in the '*Selling creativity*' section below. For the moment, it is enough to be aware that this is, and will remain a common reaction, particularly in 'hands dirty' management like engineering and facilities.

A Pygmalion technology

'As the births of living creatures at first are ill-shapen, so are all innovations, which are the births of time.' *Francis Bacon, sixteenth-century philosopher*

Creativity is a classic example of a Pygmalion technology. If those involved in creativity believe they are going to achieve something, they will. If the process is undertaken in an air of cynicism, with the feeling that it has all been seen before, there will be little practical outcome. Perception is very important to creativity in a number of factors. The perception that:

- Management believes this is worthwhile – put your money where your mouth is.
- This is not just another fad – innovation has to become part of the culture, not a nice-to-have for a few weeks after attending a course.

- It works – an early demonstration of a reliable creativity technique in action is essential to weaken the cynics' position.
- It is not a trendy (US/West Coast) theory, getting in the way of real work – an element of background can help here, pointing out that creativity is not (had better not be) the sole property of anywhere, and that this a real tool for real work.

It is because of this Pygmalion nature that many creativity sessions are part training and part practical exercise. It is fine to launch into a creativity technique when all those present are familiar with what creativity can deliver but, even when the technique is easy to use, many newcomers will benefit from some introductory material to encourage a positive view of the approach.

This Pygmalion effect extends beyond the mere acceptance of creativity to the actual development of ideas. If we think that a problem is insoluble, or there is not a product to be found in a particular area, we do not get very far with a solution. If, on the other hand, we know that someone else has solved a problem or produced a product, it must be possible and we will find a way – even if it is a totally different way – forward. Time and time again, inventions and solutions have resulted from misunderstanding. In fact, given the right circumstances it can make a very practical creativity technique. Let the team know that a different company has achieved a particular requirement, and a little bit about what they have achieved, but nothing about how. Time and time again, a solution will emerge where before it was thought impossible.

The following are just a few examples where the knowledge that someone else has made an achievement (whether or not it was true) has resulted in an innovative development:

Pygmalion innovation

Louis XVI of France was delighted by the Montgolfier brothers' balloon. He wanted one of his own, and ordered his pet scientist, Jacques Charles to make one. Charles had not seen the Montgolfier balloon, and not realizing that it used hot air to gain lift, devised a whole new class of balloon using newly discovered hydrogen.

Alexander Graham Bell's development of the telephone was an attempt to reproduce Johann Reis's work. Bell did not realize, thanks to the problems of translating from German, that Reis had not made any attempt to use his device to carry speech, and so went far beyond what he thought he was imitating.

The electron microscope as now used was developed as a result of a form of misunderstanding. Reading of the development, a physicist devised three different ways the microscope could work. One of these has proved by the far the best. He later discovered that the original invention used one of his other concepts, not the best one.

What is wrong with suggestion schemes?

'Creativity can **dramatically** improve the performance of the "human" functions (rather than the process functions) of an organization: product design, R&D, marketing and HR are good examples of "human" functions, where the performance of one or two individual brains is really important.' *Mark Adams, Director, Text 100 plc*

A classic response from the 'coalface' to the discussion of systematic creativity is, 'Why do we need this creativity business? We've already got a suggestion scheme'. There was a time when the staff suggestion scheme was the beginning and the end of an innovation agenda in most companies. The theory seemed good. Anyone in the company could contribute a suggestion. When they had a bright idea (or brain wave, or whatever glossy term was chosen for the scheme), they filled in a form, popped it in the post and before long the best ideas would be implemented, with the idea merchant awarded a nice, fat cash bonus.

It has been recognized for a long time that suggestion schemes are not very effective, given the resource available and the meagre results they generally produce. What is now being suspected is that suggestion schemes in their traditional format are actually disadvantageous. It is not that they are harmless but useful; they can be destructive.

The suggestion scheme problem has many causes. The administration of such schemes is a thankless task. Generally it is given a low administrative priority. So it can take a long time for an idea to be processed – sometimes so long that the idea is no longer current. When the idea comes to be assessed, there is often a natural reluctance from the assessor to accept it. A classic reaction is 'we've tried it/thought of it before and it didn't/won't work'. The trouble is, this kind of assessment totally overlooks the point that most new ideas are easy to shoot down. They need to be nurtured, not assessed into an early grave.

The negatives do not end there. Many schemes set the level of award on a proportion of the cost-saving the idea generates. At a stroke this disenfranchises any ideas that involve revenue enhancement rather than cost-cutting. In fact, it generates a mind-set that cost-cutting is more important than revenue generation – a fatal position if a company is to survive and grow. To add insult to injury, many schemes distinguish between manager and worker, or between areas of the company. Managers are not allowed to take part because 'it's their job to have ideas'. Yet an engineer who thinks of a way of reusing a flange sprocket instead of buying a new one (surely his job too) gets a fat cheque.

The outcome is a system that is divisive, generates negative feeling and stresses costs over revenue. This does not mean that it is impossible to get creative input from the entire company. Quite the reverse. Just that the suggestion scheme is not an appropriate vehicle. This chapter looks at a number of ways of making innovation a part of the company culture. To support that, ideas from the staff need to be encouraged. But they should be able to work outside of a formal scheme, sending them directly to those who can make it happen, or to their manager if they do not know who to send it to. Effective use of e-mail within the company is probably the strongest vehicle for making this happen. If there is a culture that it is acceptable to send an e-mail to anyone – the chief executive included – with an idea or suggestion, ideas will flow from the most unexpected sources.

While researching this book, I contacted a number of large companies, asking what they did to further creativity and innovation in the company. One multinational gave a good example of why suggestion schemes do not work. To avoid embarrassment, the company is referred to below as X:

Getting it wrong

The company's PR department, on a second contact said: 'I found this on the intranet – I didn't even know we had anything like this.' What she referred to was a document explaining the suggestion scheme. The document had all the right buzzwords, but it managed to make innovation about as exciting as filling in an expenses form. For example: 'To gain and sustain competitive advantage, X must stay ahead of the field in innovation as well as cost reduction and efficiency. All employees have a part to play in identifying new practices etc. to enhance revenue generation, improve the way the company operates and maximize continuous improvement.' Just in case the wrong people got hold of the document: 'The arrangements explained in this document are for all employees of X plc. Non-X people may offer suggestions: they will not receive awards if their suggestions are used, but their contribution will be recognized.'

There then follows the usual painful process of suggestion scheme mechanics. It is interesting that there is a creativity technique called 'Reversal' where, in order to solve a problem, you first try hard to make the opposite happen. For example, when trying to improve communications in a company, you first say what would positively discourage communications, then turn round the ideas that arise to stimulate positive communication. This scheme shows every sign of reversal being used without ever turning things back round. For example, could you think of a better way to make sure that contractors and other non-permanent staff did not think of themselves as part of the company, and did not have buy-in to what the company was trying to do?

Reward should not be through a separate scheme, implying that creativity is something special you do once in a lifetime, but through the regular company reward scheme. See more on rewarding innovation in Chapter 9. It should not be a case of 'we can give you a cash bonus because having this idea isn't your job'. Instead, having an idea has to be everyone's job, and those who do it well need to be rewarded appropriately, just as they are rewarded for other aspects of their job.

Ideas Olympics

A related idea to the suggestion scheme that has become popular in a number of other countries, but has not made much penetration in the UK is the 'ideas Olympics'. This is a (typically annual) event with an all-out attack on ideas in a concentrated space of time. The ideas Olympics holds some of the same dangers as a suggestion scheme. Unless it takes place alongside reward for creativity, it still devalues ideas generated as a normal part of the job. However, the special event razzmatazz does lift it out of the rut that the suggestion scheme has fallen into.

It is interesting that the typical examples of success in ideas Olympics are almost always from engineering-based firms. The Norwegian marine engineering giant Kvaerner claim considerable success, while in Japan, Toyota has an annual idea fest which can be stunningly productive (though this has to be seen in the context of the Japanese business environment, where suggestion schemes pull in many, many more entries than in Western countries). Moving outside industry, Expo 2000 in Hanover will feature an ideas Olympics – but again very much in a technology- and engineering-driven framework. An idea submission process seems to fit well with the engineering mentality (and with engineering problems).

In the end, it is the excitement of a big event that produces the effectiveness of an ideas Olympics. As such, it is a useful weapon for helping build a climate of creativity, particularly it seems in engineering firms, but it can never replace the value of everyday creativity in the workplace.

Selling creativity

'People wish to be settled: only as far as they are unsettled is there any hope for them.' *Ralph Waldo Emerson, nineteenth-century philosopher*

Mona, the Operations Manager, did not have many good words for creativity (or management training in general). There will always be some people who will never come to terms with anything they have not been doing for the last twenty years, but they are relatively few and far between. (They are also very dangerous people to have as managers in the modern climate of change and flexibility. Perhaps it is time to consider a different career path?) Each of the negative points that Mona made can be countered by sensible argument, coupled with an overall justification of the need for creativity.

When selling creativity, begin by establishing the need. See Chapter 1 for more detail, but the need to cope with constant change, ever better competitors and ever more complex problems will convince most people that creativity is necessary (even if it is a necessary evil). What then is needed is to establish that the particular approach taken – the creativity techniques devised by the business creativity community – is the right way forward. Look at some of Mona's complaints:

- It is fine for marketing, but not for managers in the real world.
- We know exactly what is needed: we do not need to be creative.
- This is an American fad.
- It involves silly games.
- It is a waste of time.
- We will go back to the office and ignore it.

It is fine for marketing, but not for managers in the real world

There is no doubt at all that marketing does require creativity, but this argument falls into the trap of assuming that creativity is something 'the creative people' do – something for the advertising agency, the marketing whizz kids, but not for the rest of the company. It is necessary to stress that creativity is not just about making fancy advertisements and silly publicity stunts. The sort of creativity we are concerned with is the creativity of every-day business, the creativity to solve a complex problem that cannot be dealt with by doing things the way we always have, the creativity to deal with a wildly changing set of requirements and the creativity to come up with fresh new ideas to keep the everyday afloat.

We know exactly what is needed: we do not need to be creative

This is a similar fantasy to the one above. It implies that, while some parts of the company are exposed to the frantic world of change, here in Information Technology/Finance/Operations/the department of your choice, we are protected from the problems of the world. We just get on with our job; it is down to someone else to handle change and unpredictability. Unfortunately, if it is true, the proponents of this theory are arguing themselves out of a job. Surely you do not need a manager if we know exactly what is needed? You just need a rule book. In practice, though, it is a fallacy. Their department is not special. It is exposed to all the threats and opportunities that buffet the rest of the company, and is equally in need of creative thinking.

This is an American fad

There is an unfortunate tendency outside the USA to regard anything imposed from the outside as a form of US imperialism. If you are US based, this one is a non-starter; elsewhere it can be a problem. In this particular instance, there is a strong argument against it, as many of the key names in creativity are not American. Certainly there are American names, but also British, Maltese, Hungarian – very much a worldwide approach. What is more, it would be hard to describe creativity as a fad. Creativity itself has been talked about for thousands of years. The techniques are based on thinking that has developed over the last forty years. This is not a new concept which will disappear like a cult to be replaced by the next new enthusiasm – creativity is here to stay.

It involves silly games

Creativity techniques often seem silly because their purpose is to divert – to push thinking away from the everyday. However, this is not silliness just for the sake of it. As Edward de Bono points out in *Serious Creativity*, creativity is quite distinct from crazy or off-the-wall behaviour for its own sake. This is planned, focused craziness. It is like the difference between a petrol engine and a petrol bomb. Both involve the explosive ignition of an amount of petrol – they are both 'crazy' actions. Yet one is planned and controlled to make a cylinder move, the other is random and destructive. Creativity techniques and silly games use the same motive power, but with a very different end.

It is a waste of time

This is the classic 'swamp and alligator' cry. Here am I, up to my neck in alligators and you want me to think about draining the swamp. It does not just apply to creativity, it is the reaction of everyone who is so busy with their labour that they do not have time to use labour-saving devices. Computer programmers, for example, have long been able to save away snippets of code to reuse them later when they have the same need. Too often, the wheel gets reinvented every time, because there 'was not enough time' to set up a code library, or pull something out of it. Similarly, when you are faced with a problem, the last thing you want to do is turn away from it and resort to a creativity technique. Yet this response is illogical. It is like trying to take off the wheel nuts of a car with your hands, because you do not have time to go to the back of the car and get out the spanner. Creativity techniques are tools to make problem-solving and idea generation quicker and easier. The investment of time in using them is repaid with generous interest. Perhaps the issue here is that you may get by without them – but you will definitely do a much better job with them.

We will go back to the office and ignore it

All too often this is the case. However, looked at rationally, is this a complaint about creativity, or about the people themselves? Creativity techniques will help in day-to-day business, but often everything learned on a course will be dropped because of the sort of time pressures referred to in the previous paragraph. This is where systematic creativity comes in: without some support for creativity in the systems of the company it is unlikely to flourish.

Selling the results of creativity

'I create, therefore I sell.' *Julian Patterson, Editor, VNU New Media*

Sometimes it is almost as difficult to sell a good idea as it is to sell the creative process. You know you have got a great scheme, but the rest of the world is not convinced. The arguments are weighty:

- It is too new.
- We do not do that kind of thing.
- It is not proven.
- It could go wrong.

Better stick with what we know, that is what these arguments amount to. Sometimes, creative output sells itself. It is so obviously right that everyone asks why it has not been done for years; it instantly becomes the common-sense choice. At other times, it is too original, too far from the obvious to be immediately popular. It can be enough, then, to use conventional selling methods. A good, well-presented proposal with well thought out arguments may be sufficient to tip the balance. But what if something more is required?

There are times when creativity needs yet more creativity in the way that it is sold. The 3M Post-it notes case study (see 'Do we need them?' in Chapter 4) is a good example. Often one of the best ways to sell an idea is to implement it in some prototype form in your spare time. A real physical product in use, or a real solution to a problem in action is much more convincing than a mere proposal. Another option is to use fear as a lever. It might not be enough to say that you have had a great idea, but what if there is a rumour around that your closest competitor, your greatest business threat, has had a great new idea or has solved the same business problem that you have. Starting a false rumour about the competition may seem sneaky, but it is a good way to get people to act. In fact, even if you do not have a new product in mind, or a solution to a problem, it can be interesting to let it be known that the opposition have already got something underway. Remember, creativity is a Pygmalion skill. If you believe that someone else can do it, then you believe you can too – and the solution will be found.

Amongst the alligators

'Creativity is vitally important to us as it's essentially how we compete with other software houses doing the same thing as ourselves. We have to be innovative in literally all that we do – otherwise someone else will have all the good ideas!' *Peter J. Morris, Technical Director and Lord of Funk, The Mandebrot Set*

Many of the best creative results come from cross-functional teams. This is hardly surprising. As innovation is driven by taking a new, fresh standpoint, it is only to be expected that a computer programmer might have a much better idea about how to change a financial product than an accountant, or an engineer may solve a sales problem better than a salesman. Cross-functional groups not only provide a wide range of expertise, they allow fresh insights into foreign territory.

Most companies have some degree of functional organization. In the 1980s it was popular to try to link these 'smokestacks', to overcome organizational boundaries. Concepts like internal customers and partnerships attempted to produce bridges between the smokestacks. Yet in practice, cross-functional teams remain an oddity, rather than the normal working structure. Fixed departmental boundaries are still the order of the day. For this reason, it makes sense to examine creativity 'at the coalface' in broad organizational terms. We will consider some prime departmental roles: strategy, sales and marketing, operations and support.

Strategy

> 'Creativity allows your company to develop potential you couldn't have imagined, in ways that you wouldn't have dreamed to achieve results that exceed all of your expectations.' *Paul Birch, Director of Runston Consulting*

If there is a single area of a company where creativity is a raw essential it is wherever the direction of the company itself is set. Whether this is done by a strategy department or senior management, strategy involves looking into the future. This is a risky business. However much the past is known and understood, the future is not known. We can make assumptions from what has happened in the past, we can forecast what is likely to happen, but whatever the outcome we are indulging in educated guesswork.

To a significant extent, this guesswork is shored up by intuition. A lot of work has been carried out on the nature of intuition without coming to any concrete conclusions. What is known is that most executives believe that intuition provides a strong input to their decision-making. Facts are all very well, but when it comes to making the key decisions, intuition will often rule the day. While there is limited evidence of what is happening when an intuitive decision is made, it seems reasonable that the decision-maker is relying on a whole host of snippets of knowledge and experience, plus any personal inclination to creativity to come up with a result.

Because of this strongly internalized approach, strategic decision-makers may find it hard to take the step into using formal creativity techniques. This is a mistake, however, as creativity can and should have a major impact on the development of strategy. Senior decision-makers may not take the time to learn techniques themselves, but will benefit significantly if they can be supported by effective creativity facilitation. Also, techniques will often be used by groups to generate and refine alternatives before presenting them to a top-level strategic group, providing the essential innovation prior to decision-making.

It does seem also that the intuitive process is helped by undertaking exercises to expand the creative ability. For this reason, workshops and seminars on creativity, and regular practise of creativity techniques is beneficial even if the techniques themselves are not regularly applied directly by the decision-makers but with the help of a facilitator.

Sales and marketing

'Anyone can be creative. But success means channelling that creativity in the context of the potential customer. To that end, the product and your target audience dictate where clever ends and "huh?" begins.' *James Beaven, PR Manager, Virgin Interactive*

If creativity is essential to deciding strategy in turbulent times, it is never more explicit than in sales and marketing. It is here that creativity is traditionally recognized. Unfortunately, the traditional assumption is that you place your creative requirements in the hands of a 'creative agency' who will do the creativity for you.

Making your company a creative one will not turn your in-house people into film directors or advertising executives. In fact, this would be a real disadvantage. Most advertising is highly uncreative. It deals with reaction, rather than innovation. If studies show that, for example, women do most of the shopping at supermarkets, supermarket advertising will usually show women shopping. Sometimes, in an explicit attempt to be creative, advertising will be wild, confusing or just downright silly. This can be very effective for grabbing attention – a prime requirement for advertising – but it can also be a turn-off. In fact, the most successfully creative advertising is the humorous. Humour is a vastly underrated side of creativity – done well, it has the dual benefit in an advertisement of getting the attention of and generating a warm feeling in the customer, which cannot be a bad thing.

Yet this talk of advertising misses the point. Television advertising (which I assumed by default in the previous paragraph) is a very predictable, uncreative approach to the need to advertise. When the marketing department starts to be genuinely creative, it will look at totally new alternatives. This does not mean television advertising loses its value but, to get the edge, you need something more – perhaps using the Internet, advertising on cows (the direct, and very powerful outcome of using a creativity technique devised by creativity consultant Michael Michalko), or something completely different. It certainly will involve other ways of reaching the customer than simply advertising. Creativity is the lifeblood of marketing – for too long, marketing departments have relied on outside agencies whose income depends on making advertisements. It is very rare that an ad agency's response to a customer is 'you don't want to advertise, you want to do this instead ... '. Some public relations agencies, like the technology PR company Text 100, are looking to move out of simply pushing out press releases and organizing events for journalists. Text 100 is advocating offering a range of services to its clients, including creativity consultancy, to ensure that the client has a wide, creative response to their requirement. But Text 100 is a rare example of difference in a uniform world.

Marketing opportunities for using creativity are diverse. How should we be developing products and brands? How should we make sure our marketing is effective – and different? How do we find/make new markets? And much more. If there was ever a department that ought to make creativity techniques a regular part of their development work, it is marketing. Of course, many marketing departments will respond by saying: 'We do use creativity techniques. We use brainstorming.' There is a problem here. Brainstorming is not a good way of coming up with original ideas. It provides no stimulation to get out of the conventional way of thinking. Brainstorming alone will not make a marketing group creative.

It might seem less obvious that creativity is a useful weapon for sales. Sales is much more concrete, less touchy-feely than marketing. But improving sales is fundamentally about the unknown. There is a limited amount that can be done by building a relationship – itself a process that requires creativity to bring small company 'touching' to a large company environment. But there is much more possible if only you can sell to some of the vast bulk of the (world) population who do not buy your products. Creative opportunities abound.

Operations

'When you need to create great software under huge time pressure, it can be very easy to become fixated on a single solution. Creative thinking techniques allow us to take a step back from the problem and develop smarter systems faster.' *Catherine Doherty, Director of InvestIT*

The operational aspects of a business are often the most rigid and codified. There is some merit in this for the everyday occurrence. Customers like consistency of service. They demand predictability where it is required. They do not want to turn up at the railway station to find that the train has been creatively rescheduled, or to walk into a store to find that they will have to wait three weeks before the product they want to buy can be delivered. Efficiency requires a degree of stability.

However, operational and customer service staff are constantly faced with challenges that require a different response. Operational management consists in large part of problem-solving. What to do when half the customer service staff phone in sick, or the computer goes down, or there is a sudden rush order that it is impossible for you to manufacture in time, or your main competitor suddenly drops prices or brings in a great new product?

Day-to-day operations need to give the appearance of smooth running, but underneath, swan-style, there is a huge amount of thrashing going on. All this need to respond to events requires a great deal of flexibility and innovation. If the sudden illness among your staff can instantly be countered by bringing in the cover you already had arranged, fine. Otherwise you need a creative solution, and quickly. Creativity techniques should be as much a part of the operational armoury as the telephone, fax and whiteboard.

Support sections

Every large company has a number of support sections – finance, information technology, human resources, purchasing, facilities – parts of the company whose role is not necessarily directly contributing to the bottom line, but whose work enables others to fulfil their frontline responsibilities. Such support sections are often low in morale, because they are regarded as second-class citizens. In a customer-focused company, these sections will constantly be reminded that they are only there on sufferance, not because they contribute to the essential core business. They will operate in an uncertain world, under regular threat of outsourcing.

Creativity can have a double value to support sections. First, such sections are under constant pressure to prove their value. Creativity can be used both to reduce the cost of the support section, and to increase its value to the company. There are few support sections that could not benefit from a creative transformation of their procedures and product range. Second, if creativity is extended to the organization (see the 'Doing it differently' section in Chapter 4), support sections move out of the shadow of the back room. In a DisOrganized company, the support sections are the frontline, in their own business. A bank's IT department is not an irritating overhead containing second-class citizens. It is an IT company that happens to work in the banking sector. It is doing frontline work for real customers – and this can mean a total transformation in both the working practices of the IT department and the service it gives to the bank.

Systematic creativity

'Creativity allows everyone in a company to contribute, think the unthinkable, be taken seriously and just possibly come up with something that will blow the minds of the customer and astonish your competitors.' *Mark Ralf, Director, BUPA plc*

What all the opportunities to make creativity work in real business come down to is the need for systematic creativity. Not creativity by rote, or creativity as part of a fifty-page form to be filled in when a new project is started, but creativity that is an inherent part of the company culture. Creativity that is just as much a part of the accepted tool kit of the business as a personal computer or a telephone.

People need to be convinced. Creativity is not approachable by normal logic. If creative solutions were the outcome of logical processes, there would be no need for creativity techniques – and creativity would no longer be a source of lasting competitive advantage. Like cost reduction it would be open to immediate copying and countering. Instead, creativity is much more valuable, but the indirect nature of the challenge means that it will require positive selling to the managers who will have to put it in place. Otherwise they are going to give it lip service, just as they have to all the other great ideas which descended from on high to get in the way of real work, and then ignore it.

Yet this need to sell creativity does not make it less valuable. To begin with e-mail (or the telephone) was considered a waste of time and a novelty. Such communication vehicles need critical mass. There is nothing more sad than being the only person with a new communication tool. Creativity needs a different sort of critical mass – the cultural acceptance that it is valuable, that the company thinks it is worth while and that creativity techniques do the job. To make all this happen, some form of systematic approach may well be initially necessary. We will see more of this in the agenda for innovation (Chapter 9), but it comes down to establishing a culture, making people aware of the availability of techniques, providing training and facilitation, and ensuring that the opportunity arises to make use of these techniques in day-to-day processes, with plenty of real-life examples of success and the sort of ideas that have arisen to make the benefits and the solidity of it all obvious.

Executive summary

- Creativity is a Pygmalion technology – practical experience is necessary to believe in its value, and without this belief it is unlikely to be used.
- Suggestion schemes are very limited sources of creativity – in fact they can devalue creativity and make it less common.

- It is necessary to sell both the practice of creativity and the outcome of creativity.
- All the activities of a company will benefit from creativity, not just the 'creative' department.

Chapter 6

A moment's pause

Before moving into action on creativity, it is worth taking a moment to step back and check your position. This chapter provides an opportunity to clarify understanding and make sure that you are starting from where you think you are.

Dos and don'ts

Creativity is not an area where you are working in certainties. If the outcomes of a problem were certain, there would be no need for a creative solution, you would just go ahead and do it. However, it is quite possible to collect together some dos and don'ts of effective innovation.

When developing a culture of creativity

Do	Don't
Sell the benefits of creativity	Force creativity as yet another formal process
Develop and tutor staff	Command and control staff
Imbue principles	Enforce rules
Encourage communication	Restrict communication
Throw away the organization chart	Rely on job descriptions
Consider DisOrganization	Try tinkering with processes, bound by the same faults
Lead by example	Say one thing and do another

When exploring the problem area

Do	Don't
Obtain a broad understanding	Try to obtain every bit of information in depth
Ask 'why' of everything	Make assumptions
Look at different ways of phrasing the problem	Take the problem as given
Consider doing nothing	Mistake action for a solution
Examine the obstacles to success	Focus only on the desired outcome
Make sure you have a clear problem statement	Assume everyone knows what has to be done

When solving problems and generating ideas

Do	Don't
Use a creativity technique	Wait for inspiration
Let ideas flow freely	Evaluate ideas as they emerge
Move away from the problem	Always keep the problem at the centre of attention
Generate many possible answers	Look for *the* right answer
Build on other people's ideas	Criticize other people's ideas
Be bold	Be restricted by practicality
Use a variety of techniques	Get in a rut with techniques
Respect the obvious	Look for a new solution when an obvious one is available
Pass useful ideas on to other people	Worry about the ideas which are not being used

When evaluating and refining ideas

Do	Don't
Pick ideas with appeal	Pick ideas on immediate practicality
Use intuition	Use logic alone
Look at the positive aspects and how to make them even better	Mix positive and negative
Look at the negative aspects and how to fix them	Simply state the negative
Consider the basic requirements to implement	Put together a detailed implementation plan
Be prepared to go back and choose again	Consider decisions cast in concrete

When implementing

Do	Don't
Use prototyping and time boxing	Use a detailed project plan
Monitor key milestones	Monitor every possible variable
Consider risk	Let risk control everything
Celebrate success and failure	Be too busy to celebrate anything
Learn from failure	Castigate failure
Feed lessons back into the process	Cover up

The reality check

Case studies are very valuable in business books. War stories bring theory to life, giving it much more impact than it could as dry concepts alone. However, it is necessary to establish a reality check when thinking about case studies. First, a case study is a moment frozen in time. Life and business go on, the case study stays, perfectly preserved on the bookshelf. Look at any ageing business book and examine the case studies. Some of the names you see will still be high in the firmament of success – others will have plunged to destruction. Second, a case study is there to make a point. It may stop at that convenient point. For example, it may describe the generation of a great new idea, the implementation of that idea and the initial positive feedback, without bothering to mention that six months later it was withdrawn because the idea did not work after the initial euphoria died down.

Finally, a case study is specific. We are used to arguing against those who say 'my business (or department or whatever) is a special case'. This is commonly used as a defence to avoid change and commitment. Yet the fact is, an approach that worked for one sector may not be so effective in another. Cross-industry fertilization is a great way to generate new ideas, but like any other creativity technique, it will generate plenty of losers too. A classic example may well be the Internet business. For several years after it became a commercial enterprise, business was scrabbling around trying to work out how to make money out of the Internet. A common approach, now appearing to be a common error, was to think 'it has some similarities to television, so we will treat it like television'. But the similarities are superficial, the difference immense – and the money wasted has run into billions of dollars.

This is not an argument against using case studies or enjoying them as a reader, but it is a warning against assuming that the specific results or approach of another company can be slavishly copied with an inevitable duplication of benefit. Just as Hollywood staggers from one copycat theme to another when a film makes big money and everyone tries to cash in on the same type of film, so businesses need to take the specifics of case studies with a pinch of salt. Yes, be impressed by the effectiveness of creativity techniques; no, do not expect the same specific results here.

Where are you now?

Except in the very few cases where you may be reading this book prior to setting up a new company from scratch, there will be a status quo. It is very helpful in knowing how to proceed with the introduction of creativity to see just where your company stands at the moment.

Creativity guru John Kao advocates a creativity audit. This involves looking at your company's results, and checking how much of your revenue comes from products and services that are (say) five years or less, three years or less and under a year old. The outcome of this survey provides a direct measure than can be used to compare with other companies. This is a starting point, but should not be taken alone. After all, it may be that you have a very consistent product – one of Kao's regular examples of creativity is Coca-Cola, whose disastrous experiment with a new recipe and the subsequent return to the classic formulation is well known. For a company like Coca-Cola, creativity has to be all about the ways it handles the product and the interaction with the customer, and less about the development of new products.

There are other measures, sometimes more qualitative, of internal creativity you can use too. How does a creative idea get from an individual into production? How is risk treated? What resources are available to support and encourage creativity? How does the organization help (and hinder) creativity? How are problems solved and new product ideas generated? What do the different departments do about being creative? The answers to all these questions will help build up a picture of creativity as it already exists. Whatever the picture, it can be bettered, but knowing the starting point is a valuable input to the process.

Beware the fulfilment ratio

An audit of a company's creative efforts is a valuable tool to help assess where you are now, but be very wary of another approach sometimes used to assess a company's creativity. This factor, sometimes known as an 'idea quotient' or 'fulfilment ratio' (FR) is the proportion of ideas which are implemented. The concept behind this measure seems to make a lot of sense. It is all too easy to come up with a great idea, then do nothing with it. One of the distinctive marks of business creativity is the stress on implementation – some go as far as to say that it is impossible to be creative without implementation: a pure idea has no value without making use of it. Using an FR provides a monitor of how ideas are being pushed through.

If the FR is examined at a surface level it seems appropriate enough. The problem is that there are two sets of figures being condensed into one, and the condensation process loses the value of the information. An exact parallel (though the condensation happened in the opposite direction) can be seen in the school league tables published by the British government in the 1990s. To give each school a position, the top A level rating of A was given a high score, B a lower score and so on. Each pupil's results were added, then the scores were averaged over the number of pupils so big schools did not have an artificially inflated result. The trouble is, that by adding the results together, the outcome was crucially dependent on the number of A levels the pupils took. By throwing in, for example, an extra A level in general studies, a school could inflate its position, even if the overall subject results worsened. The measure used was flawed, because it did not allow for, or convey, the number of examinations taken.

The FR suffers from a similar problem. It does not take into account the number of, or quality of, ideas generated. On FR alone, a company that had one idea to reduce the number of paperclips it used will sit smugly with a ratio of 1.0, while a company which had a hundred ideas, twenty-five of which were used (totally transforming the company's profitability) would be nursing a ratio of 0.25. Remember the difference between quality control and creativity. Quality control, aiming for zero defects is great for production, but hopeless for development. Good creativity will mean lots of useless ideas, lots of ideas which fail – with essential learning along the way – and plenty of great ideas to implement. But inevitably those implemented ideas will be in the minority. If you take measuring idea output seriously, it is essential to monitor both the number of ideas produced and the number of implementations, not just a ratio. Even better, measure the degree to which creativity is part of the culture, and the ideas will look after themselves. See the checklists in the next section.

Checklists for action

In Chapter 9 we will be looking at the actions needed to bring creativity into a company. These checklists could sit equally well there, but as some belong to the preparatory stage rather than the action stage, they have been collected here. The checklists are a set of actions or questions to be answered, as a result of which you should have a better picture of your current status and what remains to be done.

Background

- Browse creativity web sites (see Chapter 10).
- Read more widely on creativity (see Chapter 10).
- Talk to companies with more activity in creativity.

Creative audit revisited

- Check product freshness in five-, three- and one-year categories.
- Describe company attitude to risk.
- List creativity support resources.
- How are new products developed?

Selling creativity

- Establish ground-swell reaction at a sufficiently low level to distinguish different types of manager/departmental culture.
- Build on the advantages seen by managers.
- Disprove the disadvantages seen by managers.
- Demonstrate practical applications.
- Use a short (one to two hours) introduction to put the benefits across practically.

The creative culture

- Check current company communications for mention of creativity/innovation.
- Establish buy-in from the top.
- Establish communication requirements to enable free flow of ideas.
- Look at e-mail, bulletin boards/Notes, intranet.
- Look at what other companies have done.
- Implement communications mechanism.
- Communicate by example from the top.
- Establish attitude to risk-taking and failure.
- Establish attitude to trust.
- Develop programme to change attitudes if necessary.
- Implement programme.
- Consider ideas Olympics.

Training

- Does your company have any creativity training in the current training schedule?
- Locate creativity trainers.
- Consider the balance of outsourcing and training in-house trainers.
- Consider the balance of departmental and companywide training.
- Arrange courses.
- Implement courses.

Resources

- Locate creativity trainers (see 'Training' above).
- Locate creativity facilitators/consultants.
- Consider the balance of outsourcing and training in-house facilitators.
- Build in-house creativity library.
- Provide staff attending courses with appropriate books.
- Ensure that time is available for personal creativity development.
- Ensure developments in communications support creativity (see 'Creative culture' above).
- Provide appropriate access to the World Wide Web.
- Consider establishing a corporate jester as a fixed-term role.
- Help staff/managers understand the value of a network of external support resources.

Systematic creativity

- Examine formal processes for points where creativity should be introduced.
- Make staff/managers aware of key points where creativity might be valuable.
- Establish a creativity section in the formal assessment scheme (if used).
- Make annual creativity awards personal and valuable.
- Give managers a mechanism for instant creativity awards for special contributions.
- Consider an innovation centre as a fixed-term start-up resource.
- Make creativity training (see 'Training' above) part of standard training programme.
- Look at your organization: consider whether it can stand up to the needs of a creative future.
- If appropriate, draw up first steps for reorganization or DisOrganization.

Chapter 7

Innovation in context

Creativity cannot exist in isolation. It fits within a family of business tools and techniques which are increasingly accepted as the requirement for managers as we move into the third millennium. This chapter examines some of the other disciplines, looking at how creativity fits alongside them, and considers the way that new developments might change creativity.

Fitting into the business armoury

'I believe that innovation is everybody's business in both senses of the phrase.' *Keith Oates, Deputy Chairman, Marks & Spencer*

Business creativity sits alongside a range of other business tools and techniques. Inevitably there is some overlap, but there is nothing else that can replace creativity. The need for innovation should be well understood now. Many other techniques aim to solve problems, but it is rare that they produce creative solutions. For this reason, while many of the techniques covered briefly in this chapter are highly effective, they need to be used alongside creativity now, not in isolation. Just as a business could once function by doing the same thing well for decade after decade, so it could once rely on good, logical business techniques. Logic is no longer enough.

The trouble is, as Tom Peters so eloquently puts it in the subtitle of his book *The Tom Peters Seminar* (Macmillan, 1994), crazy times call for crazy organizations. This does not mean wearing silly hats or doing silly things (though these may help some people), but rather that it is no longer enough to use the same old, tried and tested business approach. The world has changed – business techniques have to change too.

Is total quality management not enough?

Total quality management (TQM) is a wonderful concept, but it is not the universal panacea that its followers sometimes seem to think it is. In the same book, Peters points out the need to go beyond TQM. The trouble is that TQM concentrates on things that have gone wrong. The idea is to minimize the number of failures, hence transforming the business. Unfortunately, concentrating on fixing things that have gone wrong is only half the story. You also have to work on things that go right. Fixing faults, reducing error rates and improving the quality of production does not introduce that vital spark of difference that makes your service or product stand out above the rest. You will produce better quality dull products – but they will still be dull.

This does not mean that quality is unimportant. Total quality management is necessary to get things right, but it is not enough. You also need to improve the quality of ideas, the quality of innovation. This cannot come out of the essentially backward-looking, crack-filling approach of TQM – there is a requirement for creativity, alongside TQM. Creativity techniques can be used to tighten up TQM itself too. They can be applied to reducing the complaint rate or cutting the number of defects, but creativity's most important application is to the positive, to giving the cutting edge of originality. Total quality management alone cannot achieve this (and makes no pretence that it can).

Operational research

Because it has been around a long time, operational research (OR – operations research in the USA) is sometimes disregarded when looking at modern management techniques. This is a profound mistake. Operational research originated in the Second World War as mechanism for improving the effectiveness of battle operations. The sort of project the early OR practitioners worked on was producing patterns of depth-charge dispersal to have the best chance of hitting a submarine.

When the war was over, OR began to be applied to business. Since then it has made steady inroads into difficult business problems. Operational research is unusual in combining a very logical, mathematical approach with problems that often involve people. The techniques of OR are often statistically based, with applications that stretch across the business spectrum. In the 1980s, one school of OR moved away from the pure mathematical approach, making greater use of computer modelling and simulation.

Operational research has been applied so widely it is difficult to come up with definitive examples of its application. It has been used to improve the effectiveness of distribution and packing, to plan layouts of buildings and production lines, to schedule aircraft and to enhance revenue management of limited capacity, variable price commodities like airline seats. Whatever the application of OR, however, it has a practical, logical, step-by-step approach.

As such it is incapable of the leaps which typify creativity, and are required by true innovation.

Operational research and creativity work particularly well together. Creativity techniques typically generate innovative ideas that do not quite work without some modification. Operational research is excellent at taking an idea and seeing how it will work out, and how it can be tuned. With creativity techniques providing the 'what shall we do?' operational research chimes in answers to the follow-up question, 'how shall we do it?' Operational research is a problem-solving technique, but addressing a different, complementary set of problems, and as such works well alongside creativity. Some OR practitioners are now undergoing creativity training to be able to apply both disciplines to a problem.

Neuro-linguistic programming and knowledge management

Neuro-linguistic programming (NLP) has been one of the most widely debated of the management skills to emerge in the latter half of the twentieth century. Based, as it is, on studies of what made the difference between excellent therapists and the rest, it is inevitably a very 'touchy-feely' approach with limited benefits in the areas of problem-solving and idea generation. Neuro-linguistic programming is a mechanism for understanding, and hence improving, modes of communication. Although there are other aspects to it, NLP is strongly dependent on the observation that much of our modelling of the way the world works is based on our senses. We describe intangibles in terms of sight ('it looks like we will succeed'), sound ('I can't hear myself think'), touch ('it feels risky') and smell ('I smell a rat'). Neuro-linguistic programming seeks to make us aware of how we are using language to communicate, analyzing the patterns and metaphors that we and others use. The intention is to improve communication, both by being aware of what we ourselves do and gaining a better insight into what others are thinking.

Whether or not much credence is put in the value of NLP beyond the work of therapists, psychoanalysts and others who have time to pore over every word used and its meanings, there is very little overlap between NLP and creativity. Neuro-linguistic programming is all about what is, rather than what might be. Creativity, whether enhanced by specific techniques or changes in the overall creativity of a company, is aimed at specific, tangible goals. Neuro-linguistic programming has a much fuzzier target, limited to the (none the less highly important) field of interpersonal communication, knowledge mapping and information filtering.

A much stronger overlap exists between NLP and the burgeoning field of knowledge management. At the personal level, knowledge management is about improving your own skills to gather information and build knowledge, and has much in common with NLP. However knowledge management also operates at an enterprise level, where it is intended to provide a vehicle for capturing expertise (usually in computer systems) in a way that makes it possible to call on that expertise whenever it is required. This aspect of knowledge management is more closely tied to artificial intelligence (see '*Artificial creativity*' below) than NLP. Unfortunately, some businesses attempt enterprise knowledge management, as a way of replacing an expensive (or ageing) expert, rather than to complement human expertise. In practice it seems that captured, codified knowledge is 'dead knowledge' – that a knowledge base is little more than backward-looking experience. As is shown in creativity time and time again, this is more of a hindrance than a help when it comes to solving new problems that require innovation. In effect, enterprise knowledge management is the antithesis of creativity.

At the personal level, knowledge management is much more supportive of creativity. Creativity techniques do not generate creativity, they merely help release the implicit creativity we all have by moving away from existing paths and the focus on a specific solution to a specific problem. A great deal of personal knowledge management is concerned with dealing with implicit knowledge, and the way this feeds into decision-making and problem-solving. However, knowledge management will always fall short of the goal because of the problem mentioned in Chapter 2. Because of the self-patterning nature of creativity, it is impossible to make a logical step forward from current knowledge to a new idea. Instead, we must be pushed into jumping. Afterwards, we can build a logical path back to where we started from. Knowledge management can recognize the value of an idea once it is established, but is of little use in generating creative ideas.

Business process re-engineering

For a short time, business process re-engineering (BPR) seemed as if it was going to be the great new hope for ailing businesses. The idea, put simply, was to take an approach similar to the systems engineering used in computer software design and apply it to business processes. Instead of trying to patch up an ailing process, take a step back. Look at what it is trying to achieve. Then redesign the process (or rather the set of intertwined processes) which are currently in place to actually meet the business requirement.

In principle, this approach has no conflict with the use of creativity techniques. It may well be that creativity techniques could help to produce redesigned processes. However, in practice the rigid, follow-the-rules approach of BPR is so locked in that it is culturally incompatible with creativity. Business process re-engineering inevitably retains many assumptions about the business and status quo, while creativity is all about challenging and disposing of assumptions. A number of major consultancies who were originally very enthusiastic about BPR, now consider it an ineffective approach. As Michael Syrett and Jean Lammiman point out in *Managing 'Live' Innovation*, '"Leanness" of the type practised by many companies in the early 1990s – cost cutting, outsourcing, redundancies and business process re-engineering – is not enough to make a company competitive. In fact, it may well end up destroying it.'

General business skills

Without obvious exception, the popular business gurus are supportive of creativity and innovation. This is an example where the context is purely complementary to the use of creativity techniques, as these general management texts do not provide specific techniques, concentrating instead on the aspects of dealing with people, trust, enthusiasm and leadership. Whether coming from the gung-ho, chaotic rush for excellence that typifies Tom Peters, or the more thoughtful British style of Charles Handy, there is a natural reinforcement between the requirements to be a business leader of tomorrow and the need for creativity. See 'Doing it differently' in Chapter 4 for more on the way Peters and Handy consider the organization must move for creativity to be a success – and to make a creative success of the organization.

Underlying the closeness between such general business smarts and creativity are two principle areas. The first is the climate for creativity. When the business gurus speak of generating an atmosphere of trust, and allowing staff the flexibility to deal with problems (and opportunities) as they arise, they are speaking of many of the same conditions which will generate a culture that supports creativity. The second is organizational. Many business writers now accept the huge gulf between a traditional organizational structure and the need to react quickly and flexibly, and to know the customer better. The same structural changes – DisOrganization, Handy's concept of subsidiarity, Peters' crazy organizations that support the new requirements of customers and staff both arise out of a culture of creativity and help bolster it.

Directions for innovation

'No one takes the lead by being the best at following – creativity unlocks the future path.' *Mark Ralf, Director, BUPA plc*

Creativity is not static. That is a good general statement – creativity is about change, you cannot innovate without altering. However, it also describes the nature of creativity itself. Our approaches to innovating within business have developed immensely over the last half-century. There is no reason to suppose that we have reached the ultimate state in theory (and we are certainly nowhere near it in practice).

The underlying concepts of innovation are unlikely to vary much. The human aspects of creativity are reasonably well understood, at least from a pragmatic viewpoint. We might not know *how* creativity works, but we are reasonably clear which buttons to push to make something happen. What is subject to change is the methodology and technology by which we generate that button push. Information technology growth will have a major input, which is covered in the next section. Other components of the creativity tool kit will continue to evolve.

For the next twenty to thirty years, creativity is likely to remain a subject that requires outside assistance. Training, consultancy and facilitation will all need help from experts but, with time, creativity will become a much more natural aspect of our working. We will no more need an expert to come in and help with everyday creativity than we need an author to come in to tell us how to write reports. (This is not to say that such areas would not benefit often from training, just that it will not be as essential as it currently is.) This does not mean that consultancy in the field will die. Even if a company has good basic creativity skills there will always be occasions when it needs more, just as it might bring in a professional writer to produce a help manual or a press release. However, in this time frame it is reasonable to expect creativity to become a much more common tool.

Part of the basis for this encroachment of creativity will be more teaching of creativity in schools and universities. Some countries already include creativity as part of their basic education, but there are many parts of the world where creativity and schools do not sit comfortably together. This will change, but gradually.

As the use of techniques grows, the techniques themselves will be refined. At the moment, most of the techniques in use are derived by playing variations on the theme of Osborn's original list. It is likely that increased used of creativity techniques and more research into the nature of creativity will generate new forms of technique.

Finally, the internalization of creativity will become more effective. As described in Chapter 3 ('Beyond techniques' section) those who make regular use of creativity techniques find themselves more and more capable of systematic creative leaps without engaging a technique. As techniques become more commonplace, we can expect a more common ability to take these leaps. This progress does not entirely replace the need for techniques – even the most creative person can benefit from and be surprised by the result of a technique – but it will mean a different approach is taken.

Information technology growth

A significant change in creativity will be the degree to which information technology supports it. We are already seeing immense benefits from the communications infrastructures of e-mail and bulletin board, Internet and intranet. As IT continues to make inroads into our everyday life, it will also continue to impact on creativity. In the short term this is liable to mean even more opportunity to get the background to a problem filled in quickly, to research alternatives and competitors, to share and build on ideas and to use random information for stimulation.

With time, too, the use of IT to directly support creativity techniques will grow. To date, mainstream software companies have not ventured into creativity software. The closest ventures have been Microsoft's dalliance with Stephen Covey's 'Seven Habits' in the first release of the personal information manager, Outlook (probably seen as a time management venture) and the use of flow charters and similar graphical packages to map ideas. There is room for a lot more. The small companies who have produced software to generate mind maps have already demonstrated how effective these have been. Similarly, there is considerable demand for freeware and shareware packages supporting creativity techniques. The availability of such packages from mainstream vendors would do a lot to increase the visibility of creativity techniques in large companies. As the different product niches become saturated, it is only a matter of time before one of the big names stumbles into creativity.

Strangely for such a human activity, in practically every area of business creativity there is likely to be increased support from IT. Information technology will never remove the need for the people aspects. In fact, there is a danger with too much reliance on IT of forgetting the very human need for trust and a climate that nurtures creativity. Just as pushing knowledge management solely into IT kills the knowledge, pushing creativity solely into IT would kill the creativity. But a hybrid combination of people and IT is likely to be the best way forward.

Artificial creativity

Although most use of IT for creativity involves everyday software, there is a branch of computing which many will tend to think of when presented with the combination of computers and creativity – artificial intelligence (AI). Science fiction has prepared us for near-human robots, computers that seem able to reason and more. Yet the realities of AI are very different – and disappointing from the business viewpoint – in most cases.

One of the problems in assessing the value of AI (and its relevance to business creativity) is that it is a very broad term, encompassing a wide range of technologies. At one extreme it covers very theoretical research into the way that the brain works and the nature of perception. At the other it reaches into the mundane application of a set of rules which is little different from a conventional computer program.

The two technologies which have seen most business application are expert or knowledge-based systems and neural networks. In a knowledge-based system, so-called knowledge engineers work with one or more experts in a particular field to record as much as they can of their knowledge (the whole field of expert systems is littered with jargon – this process is referred to as eliciting knowledge). As much as possible, the expertise is then codified into a computer program which should be able to reproduce part of the expert's performance.

The problem with expert systems, as is made clear in *Honing Your Knowledge Skills* (Butterworth-Heinemann, 1998) by Mariana Funes and Nancy Johnson is that a lot of inaccurate assumptions were made about them in the early days. When the knowledge-based system trade was booming, the hope in business was that it would be possible to replace expensive experts with cheap, twenty-four-hour-a-day computers. This was an undesirable pipe dream. Knowledge is not the same as information. Knowledge cannot be extracted, isolated and stored for future use; it is a live, active commodity. As such the knowledge of an expert cannot be extracted, but it can be supplemented, and knowledge-based systems have found a niche supporting experts rather than replacing them. At best, knowledge-based systems can help with a diagnosis or replace a tedious rule book, but they provide no insight into artificial creativity, as they are entirely backward looking.

The second technology, neural networks, is based on the way the brain itself may work. A neural network consists of a set of 'nodes', points which are linked to many other nodes in the network. When a signal enters the network it passes through various nodes, which modify it before passing it on. If such a network can alter the weightings it applies to various paths, depending on the input, it can 'learn' from experience. The clearest application of a neural network is pattern recognition, whether identifying a picture or writing, or picking up a pattern in historical data. This is in many ways a more flexible and brain-like technology but, even so, the neural network is not a contender for artificial creativity because it is dependent on looking for existing patterns, not devising something new.

There may come a point where a technological breakthrough makes true artificial intelligence, and hence true artificial creativity. For the moment, though, all a computer can do is to provide an enormous well of information to inspire human creativity (such as the World Wide Web), to catalyse human creativity through random stimulation, and to help structure and process the ideas that are generated by people.

Executive summary

- Innovation fits well with many popular business techniques.
- A few business techniques (sometimes fads) run counter to creativity. Usually these are techniques which are fine when confined to a specific aspect of the business, but cause problems if applied too generally.
- Many general business theories implicitly incorporate innovation.

- We are going to see more explicit consideration of creativity in education and in business.
- Information technology will have a growing role, but will continue to be a support to human creativity rather than a replacement, just as it is supporting the development of knowledge rather than replacing the human element.

Chapter 8

Innovation SWOT

Innovation and creativity are not items that appear on a conventional business plan. This short chapter assesses the strengths, weaknesses, opportunities and threats of making creativity an explicit part of your company's aims. This is not an attempt at a rigorous SWOT analysis, but will provide a useful overview of the potential impact of a creative focus. It is often difficult to be clear just what is a threat or a weakness, or to distinguish between opportunities and strengths. The importance of SWOT is to obtain an overview, not to spend too long agonizing over the right choice.

Strengths

'The history of business is littered with creativity. The history of business failures is not.' *Julian Patterson, Editor, VNU New Media*

- Greatly increased capability to cope with change.
- Direct competitive advantage by finding solutions and new ideas the competition cannot.
- Much wider opportunities for new products and services.
- Solves otherwise intractable business problems.
- Repeatable, effective idea generation rather than waiting for inspiration.
- The only sustainable competitive advantage.

Weaknesses

'Creativity can wreck a company. There are many points where it's not required, where it's destructive – where order, control, predictability, precision should and do rule the roost.' *Mark Adams, Director, Text 100 plc*

- Creativity should be applied to business processes, but *constant* tinkering will unnerve staff and lead to inconsistent results.
- Increased risk. This is valuable if risk is managed and understood, but risk has to be minimized in safety critical environments.
- Some great ideas are so different that they cannot be sold into an organization (they need to be taken somewhere else).
- Creativity often happens at a middle level and is passed to the top for approval or disapproval. This can result in misunderstandings.

Opportunities

'Good software engineering is about method and experience, but to develop excellent software requires flair and creativity. Don't let the perspiration blind you to the need for inspiration.' *Phil May, Director, Data Connection Ltd*

- To improve business processes.
- To improve organizational effectiveness.
- To solve business problems.
- To come up with genuinely original ideas.
- To improve profitability.
- To reduce product/service development time.
- To increase product/service value.
- To reduce costs.
- To transform the organization to provide small company responsiveness and flexibility with large company penetration.
- To improve job satisfaction of employees.
- To enhance the company's image – being known as innovative is a significant advantage.
- Staying ahead of the sigmoid curve (see 'Handy's curve' below)

Handy's curve

In *The Empty Raincoat* (Arrow, 1995), Charles Handy points to the importance of being ahead of the sigmoid curve. Handy's contention is that the curve portrays all of life, whether it is the life of a person, an empire or a company. There comes a point where decline sets in (see Figure 8.1).

However, this is not the end of everything. There is every opportunity to restart on another curve. The trouble is that the natural tendency is to wait until you are well into decline before taking action – around point B (Figure 8.1). By then, all the indicators are there; change is an obvious requirement. However, by that time it may well be too late. Those in charge have clearly been responsible for the decline, goes the argument, so they are not the right

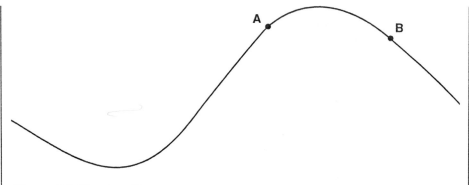

Figure 8.1 The sigmoid curve

people to lead us out of it. A new curve may well be established, but only after revolution and bloodshed.

If, however, it is possible to pick up around point A on the curve, Handy points out that you are ideally placed. You will still take a small dip from the initial drop in the curve, but before long the effect will be continuous improvement. The only problem here is a similarity with the old rule of how to make your millions on the stock market – all you have to do is buy low and sell high. Identifying when that point is reached is a lot harder than noticing that you have slipped well over the edge. What is more, convincing people of the need for change at that point is very difficult. It is the antithesis of 'if it ain't broke, don't fix it'. To really pick up on the sigmoid curve requires action before common sense says it is required – making the uncommon sense of creativity a real bonus.

Threats

> 'Creativity in business – i.e. breaking the mould, or going your own way, or reinventing your medium – is a high-risk strategy. If you win, the pay off can be grand, but mostly the go-for-broke creative mavericks lose.' *Michael Wolff, journalist and former Internet entrepreneur*

- While innovation is generally positively received (e.g. 3M, ABB) and improves a company's image, the use of creativity techniques can be maliciously or ignorantly misinterpreted as being silly, frivolous or non-businesslike.

- If innovation is introduced in a half-hearted manner, without clear support from the top of the organization, it will result in nothing but confusion and irritation.
- The biggest threat is not taking on creativity as part of the day-to-day function of the business – without it, survival is at risk.

Pulling it together

This SWOT is only useful as a tool if each of the inputs is acknowledged. We need to bear in mind the risks attached to being creative and take steps to minimize these, but we also need to make sure that the opportunities are taken into account in our business plans. It is all too easy to include only the negative in a business plan, as often the negative is easier to quantify. Costs are easier to handle than benefits – weaknesses and threats can sometimes be easier to consider than strengths and opportunities.

When talking about risk, venture capitalists often point out that the market risk is much more worrying than the technology risk. Of course, some technologies will fail to deliver, but we know that with the right people in the right environment a fair number of them will succeed. What is much less subject to certainty is the way the market will react – selling becomes a prime tool of risk management. There is something of a parallel in the field of creativity.

There is no doubt at all that the technology is capable of delivering. The human brain is hugely creative. The techniques that have been developed over the last forty years will deliver repeatable, beneficial results. However, the whole exercise can be destroyed if the value of creativity is not sold properly. It is not that creativity itself is denigrated; (almost) everyone accepts the value of creativity itself. Yet without appropriate selling, taking the time and money to develop creativity and to use creativity techniques can and will be regarded as frivolous, especially at cost-cutting times, which are the times when companies need creativity the most. Selling the strengths and opportunities of systematic creativity at all levels of the company is essential if the market risk is to be overcome.

Chapter 9

Innovation agenda

Building an agenda for innovation is not a trivial exercise. Each of the components is valuable in its own right, but there is such strong interlinking that many will not survive for long without the others – or cannot even start without a complementary piece of the jigsaw being put in place. It is hard to build a culture of innovation without a move away from management towards leadership. Creativity techniques can be introduced to the business processes, but will rapidly fall into disuse without the right resources and without innovation being part of the reward process. The culture itself is dependent on enhanced communication and breaking down the hierarchy, which threaten to start off a move to DisOrganization.

If this prognosis is frightening, it ought to be. Turning an everyday company into an innovative leader is not a minor change. It is not an incremental improvement. As Tom Peters says in *The Tom Peters Seminar*, it is a matter of revolution. This is not to say that there is no benefit to be had from the small starts of improving communications, fostering a creative culture and introducing creativity techniques. They are all worthy and worth while. But to sustain the benefit and turn creativity into a vehicle for survival and success there has to be an understanding that the company will be turned on its head.

Institutionalizing innovation

'Creativity is the essence of success in the wallpaper business in terms of the design of the product, but more importantly in providing new solutions to the everyday problems we face. Creativity in this context is a combination of "newness" and relative effectiveness – in other words, a "creative" solution, for me, is one that is both different from *and* better than those that have been tried before.' *Peter Dumigan, Marketing Director, Imperial Home Decor Group (UK) Ltd*

We have seen how an essential start to making an organization creative is building a culture that encourages creativity. Unfortunately, culture-building is not something that is achieved by a traditional campaign. You can put up all the posters you like proclaiming that 'we are a creative culture' or 'we value innovation', but cultural changes depend profoundly on the actions of the company and a flow of consistent messages from senior management. Many of the subsequent sections in this chapter will help build the innovation culture – make it part of the every day life of the company.

This does not mean that there is nothing that can be done up front. Take a quick creativity culture audit now. Browse through your recent internal briefings, in-house magazines, intranet pages – how much can you find about creativity? How often do you read about examples of the company valuing creativity, or just examples of creativity in action? Start to push the creative message into your internal communication vehicles. A few weeks of laying the groundwork will make it easier when you begin on the first concrete, very dramatic step of destroying the staff suggestion scheme.

Dismantling the suggestion scheme

'I recall reading that creative people are better able to live with inconsistent and contradictory pieces of "world model" while they explore new possibilities. I instinctively agree with this, though I confess I have no experimental support. I do find that in my business of getting people to be more adventurous, be they scientific researchers or business managers, I am often faced with the opposite. I say "Suppose A" and they say "But B". I say "What if X" and they say "But Y".' *Bob Malcolm, director Ideo Ltd*

If your company does not have a suggestion scheme, this is an easy stage in the agenda – nothing to do. However, it is a shame, because your attitude to the scheme makes a significant point. It is time to dismantle it. Very publicly – you are making a statement. Announce the end of the scheme. Look back over the scheme and celebrate its successes – but also point out where it has failed to deliver.

Make a point of emphasizing that the action is being taken not to reduce creative input from the workforce, but by making creative input part of everyone's everyday job. There is not a job in the company which does not benefit from creativity or have an input to how the company develops. To bring out the demolition of the old, consider an event where the vast mountain of suggestion forms and assessment forms and all the paraphernalia of the suggestion scheme are burned. However, do not leave these negative images as the outcome in people's minds.

To move forward, start by celebrating past successes. Then point to the ways everyone can contribute ideas – direct to the person who can make use of them via e-mail or, if they do not know who to send them to, via their boss. All managers take on the responsibility for making sure those ideas reach the right person within one working day. If you like the idea, announce the first Ideas Olympics at the same time, but do not think this can be the sole replacement of the suggestion scheme – it is just the icing on the cake.

As a final step in pulling down the old scheme, it is essential to be able to announce the content of the next step at the same time: making innovation part of the reward process. You need not have the reward structure in place immediately, but you should be able to announce its development and, crucially, when it is going to begin. Remember, creativity is stifled by discipline in inputs, but is enhanced by discipline in outputs – attach a date to the scheme, and meet it.

There is one more thing to say to the staff at this point, again about the reward scheme. If your company already has performance-based pay, emphasize that this is a new element on top of the traditional aspects, but most of all, emphasize that it will be a significant element. You may not have decided the nature of the scheme – whether, for example the reward is in the form of cash or physical goods – but good creativity is going to be rewarded with thousands of pounds rather than hundreds, or a personal computer rather than a pocket calculator.

Making innovation part of the reward scheme

We have already discussed in Chapter 4 (see 'Innovation resources' section) the need to bring creativity explicitly into the reward scheme. Now it is time to make it happen. Bringing in a change to a reward scheme is not trivial. It often involves negotiation with unions as well as persuading the board that this is not yet another way to lose the company money without any material gain. Even so, this change ought to be made reasonably quickly. If not, the company is not seen to be 'putting its money where its mouth is'. 'Do as I say, not as I do' is not a tenable stance for fostering creativity.

Begin with the nature of the reward. It does not have to be cash. In fact, ideally it probably will not be. A gift, if properly chosen, will have a much greater impact than cash. For example, against a £30 000 salary, a £300 bonus is chicken feed. No one is going to object to it, but equally they are not going to get excited or motivated. However, compared with a typical £20 watch, a £200 watch is something special. It is something to be treasured, something you remember every day. By giving someone a £200 watch or its equivalent you can both save money and have an order of magnitude bigger impact on the recipient. Everyone wins.

Moving to Mars

A good illustration of the remarkable effectiveness of gifts in comparison with financial reward can be seen in the real-life example of a manager who moved to the Mars confectionery group from another major corporate. At Christmas, the company gave him an attractive clock as a Christmas present. His wife was very impressed. 'X [his previous firm] never did that for you,' she pointed out.

'True,' said the manager, 'but at X I used to get a week's extra pay in December as a Christmas bonus. That was worth a lot more.'

His wife was not impressed. 'It's not the same,' she said.

Of course giving a gift carries an implication. It has to be appropriate for the person. There is no point giving someone who hates sport a bag of golf clubs or a football season ticket. Do not think that the easy way out is to give the recipient a catalogue to choose from, or a voucher from a big store. Everyone knows the different feel between getting a voucher for their birthday or a well-chosen present. The voucher may be worth just as much, but it is still money. The added value in a gift is the 'well-chosen' part of the description. So who is going to choose? Perhaps there should be a special gift-chooser role in the HR department? Think again. The choice has to come from the recipient's manager. Of course, that means you have to know quite a lot about your staff but that should hardly be a disadvantage, and there is genuine pleasure in giving a desirable gift, even if the company has paid for it.

There is a trap to watch out for when giving a gift. It is not an excuse to be stingy. Yes, you will be able to save money on an equivalent cash reward, but a big contribution is still going to deserve a big gift. If you can trace a direct link between an individual's creative input to the company and a £5 million profit, it is hardly profligate to give them a holiday in the Seychelles or a car. The important thing here is not to get tied up in a system – we are not trying to re-create the suggestion scheme in a different guise. Do not try to produce a table linking creative input to gift value. Apart from anything else, you will find it very difficult to quantify the value of every input. But you should have an intuitive feel for what seems right to be a genuine reward to that individual – provided, once again, that you really know her or him.

So far, so good. You have decide the nature of the reward. Now there are matters like tie in to the staff assessment scheme, frequency and how the award is allocated and funded. We saw in Chapter 4, in the 'Rewarding innovation' section, a suggestion for how creativity could become part of a formal assessment scheme. Adding in such a section should not cause much pain, but be careful how the assessment transfers to the reward. There might be a temptation if other aspects of the scheme have an automatic link to reward to carry this through to creativity, or to lump the creativity award in with the rest of the year's incentives. Do not do this. Unless the award is clearly distinguished it will have no real benefit, and you are not going to achieve a personal reward, something of real value, unless it is chosen by a person rather than a computer.

This leads to something of a quandary. The whole point of automated reward schemes that link pay rises and bonuses to quantified (and often normalized) performance measures is to remove inconsistency between managers. If the creativity award is to be at the manager's gift, how are you to be sure he or she is getting it right? The simple answer is, you are not. We are back to trust. If you have hired staff because they are good managers, it is not exactly displaying confidence in them to say you do not trust them to decide fairly on a creativity award. Yes, sometimes they will get it wrong, but this contrasts with most automated schemes which can be guaranteed to get it wrong every time.

If the size of the award is at the manager's discretion, where is the control? Apart from the fact your managers had better not be wasting company money, there is nothing to stop them being allocated a pot of money for creativity awards. This can be an absolute limit (although the limit should be considerably more than you would normally expect, to allow for special cases like a car), within which the manager has freedom to operate. Changes to the limit from year to year are probably best managed by an inversion of the old approach to budgeting. It used to be traditional in many large companies that a department that underspent its budget was allocated less next year – the way to keep your budget was to spend up to the mark. A more appropriate (and creative) approach is to say the more you underspend, the more extra budget you are allocated (as you obviously are capable of control).

This discussion has been referring to 'an' award – in fact, the pot must cover two demands. Each year, as a result of the creativity assessment, there is an opportunity for an annual award, but it is equally important that a specific act of innovation is rewarded within days. Such special one-off rewards will typically carry significantly less value than an annual award, but are equally important to stress the significance the company (and the manager) gives to creativity.

Managing for innovation

'An innovative business is one which lives and breathes "outside the box". It's not just about ideas. It's a combination of good ideas, motivated staff and an instinctive understanding of what your customer wants, and then combining these elements to achieve outstanding results.' *Richard Branson*

Encouraging creativity requires a different style of management. As described in Chapter 4, in 'Leadership versus management', this involves more leadership than traditional management. Without such a change, none of the other steps in this agenda can succeed. However much enthusiasm there is for creativity, however many resources available, however creativity is rewarded, if the managers are actively discouraging innovation it simply will not happen.

A big problem here is that the management skills required for leadership are different from those for traditional management. There are some overlaps, but there is a very different approach: the coach rather than the director, 'do as I do' rather than 'do as I say', establishing principles rather than setting rules. This style of management requires much more communication and openness. Staff should understand what their manager's priorities and goals are, getting as much feel for the 'why' of a requirement as the 'what'. For many existing managers, this is going to involve retraining. For some it is going to involve severance. It is a painful fact that some of your managers will probably never cope with the need to manage for innovation, and they should be looking for positions in companies which have yet to discover the value of creativity.

Leadership is not just a matter of training. Managers will need the right tools for the job, many of them provided by other steps in this agenda. They will also need support from above. Organization charts are sometimes printed upside down to emphasize the importance of the frontline workers, and to suggest that management's role is to support their reports. Often this is just a gimmick – there is nothing done differently. To encourage good managing for innovation there has to be more than that. Senior management has to be prepared to support the line managers – most importantly, by example. Not only do managers have to become leaders, so do the top people in the company. All too often schemes for management change have foundered because the people at the top were saying 'this is the way you should behave' without taking on the principles themselves. This approach just will not work.

Organizing for innovation

'The most promising development in our own work at Manchester is the discovery of a "two barrier" theory of group work. Most working groups pass through a standard performance barrier, while a few exceptional groups pass through a "breakthrough barrier". This gives a new group theory of form, storm, norm, perform, and outperform. The breakthrough process is a good indicator of what might define the creative group or organization.' *Tudor Rickards, Professor of Creativity and Organizational Change, Manchester Business School*

Organizing for innovation is not about setting up an innovation centre or the post of innovation manager, but requires a much more radical change. If creativity is truly to be an integral part of the company, the chances are the company is going to change in a big way. As we saw in Chapter 4, this is liable to involve very significant changes which will not happen over night. All that is necessary at this stage in the agenda is to consider the implications and the benefits of a major organizational change. Which direction should you be going in? What steps do you need to take to plan the new shape of your organization. It is possible that the outcome of this exercise is to decide that the current organization is fine as it is – but this is unlikely, and you will not know for certain until the work is carried out.

It may seem that this agenda action is totally out of proportion to the driving need. How can it be possible to justify turning the whole organization on its head just to make it creative? That is fine, if you regard creativity as the icing on the cake, a nice-to-have that will help tinker here and fine-tune there. If, however, you regard creativity as an essential requirement for survival and the prime weapon of competitive advantage, a position that is supported by most management experts these days, a change in the shape of the organization is a small price to pay for survival.

Getting innovation into processes

'Problems cannot be solved by thinking within the framework in which the problems were created.' *Albert Einstein*

This action is easier if you have already gone through a process of business process re-engineering, or business modelling. If you have not, the first step is to understand just what your business processes are. This does not have to be in the fine detail of a process model – just a list of the key processes which keep the business in action. How do you deal with a demand for your products and services? How do you ensure that there is stock to meet it (or expertise, or whatever your company deals in)? How do you solve a problem that threatens your business? How do you come up with new products and services? How do you establish a one-off project? And so on. It should be possible in an hour or so to produce a list of these key processes.

Now see how creativity should fit into each process. Is it relevant at all? Should creativity techniques be employed, and if so, where and by who? The outcome of the exercise should be a set of entry points for creativity into the process. It does not make sense to formalize the involvement of creativity by setting up rules that 'a technique must be applied before filling in section 3.51 of the form', but it is essential to indicate to those responsible for the processes that there is a need for creativity at this point, and to repeat this message throughout the period of building the creativity culture.

As you are working through the processes, with creativity in mind, feel free to be creative about the processes themselves. Although the prime aim of this exercise is not to re-engineer processes, there is no reason to avoid the opportunity if it arises. Many of the processes are liable to change radically if the outcome of the previous action is to be a revolution in organization, but it does not do any harm to spot the areas for attack. Consider the classic 'no action' creative solution. What would happen if you did not undertake the process at all? Use a creativity technique to explore alternatives to the process. Does the process itself hinder creativity? What could be done about it? Systems and processes are set up to protect the company and achieve smooth running, but after a while the arteries harden and progress is actually stifled, so it does not do any harm to re-examine these essential lifelines of the company.

Want a centre?

> 'Businesses often forget that their business isn't business. It is
> always the creation of value. Don't waste time measuring the value,
> get on and create it.' *Henry Berry, director, Theory B*

At about this point in the agenda you need to be considering whether or not you should start up a formal innovation centre. It is unlikely that you will require a permanent centre. Its presence can give the impression that creativity is not something everyone needs; it can be left to the 'experts' in the centre. Even worse, when cash gets tight at some point in the future, someone is bound to suggest shutting down the centre – and what messages will that give about the company? In the longer term, creativity resources can be handled by whoever deals with your other learning requirements. But it is worth considering a short-term centre.

A short-term centre will have a known lifetime (perhaps nine months or a year), during which it will act as a catalyst for creativity. It will ensure that training, educational materials, facilitators and other resources are made available to the company – and that the managers and staff do not forget about creativity when dealing with swamps and alligators. By the end of its lifetime (an ending that should be celebrated) the corporate culture of creativity should be established, and the centre will have served its purpose.

Training for innovation

> 'From my personal research on creativity, my work with clients on
> marketing strategies, my teaching experience as MBA professor, and
> in giving seminars on creativity, I came to the following conclusion:
> true creativity is self-encounter.' *José Ferrandis, Marketing
> Management Consultant, Ferrandis and Partners (Madrid)*

Establish a training strategy for creativity. Creativity is not a natural activity – it is more about uncommon sense than common sense. It is not enough to assume that staff and managers will pick it up as they go along – they will need training. Depending on the size and structure of the company, this can involve direct training of all staff or a 'training the trainers' approach, where a number of staff within the company are given a higher level of creativity training. In the former case a one-day course should be sufficient. For training the trainers a three-day course would be a sensible target, provided it is accompanied by practical experience alongside an experienced practitioner.

However training is arranged, make sure that secondary training resources are widely available. If possible, use a training course which provides the participant with an in-depth, practical book on creativity. If not, consider buying such books for all staff, or at a minimum having a good stock of the books available from a training library. It is also useful to have specific techniques available on call – if you use a bulletin board system like Lotus Notes, or an intranet, consider having a techniques section there. There are more resources to consider though.

Lining up the resources

'The information age has brought with it the age of bewilderment, where things themselves are no longer as important as the possible connections between things – and imagining and building new connections is the realm of creativity. Holistic, creative thinking is becoming a source of competitive edge.' *David Firth, Consultant*

In the early stages of taking on creativity, you are liable to need more external assistance in the form of consultants and facilitators. Specifically, when arranging creativity sessions involving high-level staff of the company or significant decisions, you may wish to bring in an experienced creativity facilitator. Over time facilitators will emerge within the company, although you will probably always want to look externally for assistance with some problems and decisions, particularly if you need to make sure that you are not falling into a company rut.

The other principle resources to consider at this stage are the electronic ones. Does everyone (yes everyone) in the company have access to e-mail? This does not mean a personal computer or terminal at every desk or working position, but for shop-floor workers there should be communal access to e-mail – a sort of cyber café in the rest room. Cross-company e-mail is essential for developing trust and support networks, and providing a vehicle to instantly alert a problem owner. Are your e-mail users linked to the wider world of the Internet? As we have seen, this opens up a much larger creative resource base, particularly if staff are encouraged to build a personal network outside the company.

Beyond e-mail, serious consideration should be given to an intranet if the company does not already have one. Intranets are now cheap to set up and provide an easy way to share information across the company. With modern software, intranets can include discussion groups where anyone can contribute. It is possible to go one step further to Lotus Notes, but the costs here rise significantly – if Notes is not already established in the company, it should not be rushed into. If Notes is already there, make good use of it. Ensure everyone has access to creativity databases.

Like e-mail, there is no excuse to exclude anyone from access to an intranet. It should be available by the same mechanisms to every member of staff. Incidentally, this extends both up and down the organization. It is still not uncommon for directors to ignore IT as something 'for the workers' – but the creativity culture has to come from the top. Access to the World Wide Web is a thornier problem. There are huge benefits to open access to the Web, but it is subject to misuse in some companies. None the less, it is an essential tool for knowledge workers, who should have direct access from their work positions. There is no reason why other staff cannot be given free access through the same vehicles as the intranet. If misuse becomes a problem, site access can be monitored to see who is looking at what – the mere knowledge that what you look at is known will usually have the desired effect.

Consider the benefits of software specifically designed to support creativity. It is generally quite cheap – it would be worth buying a broad set of software and finding products which particularly fit with the company's need. At this point consider a site licence – if the product really works for your company, it should be ubiquitous.

Looking at recruitment

'Our technical tests, which each prospective hire must sit, challenges them to think "around" the problem in front of them – to see through it in a creative way, to ask questions: "what's the questioner getting at here – it seems so straightforward". People who want to know how it works, why it works – those that ask to see the answers after the tests give us a good feeling – they're keen to learn which means typically that they're curious by nature. Something that you cannot switch off. It's this kind of person who'll always be running a "background thread" hunting for new ways to improve how we build software. Once you have that type of person on board and a forum and system whose sole purpose it is to nurture and encourage them to share their ideas, you're on to a winner.' Peter J. Morris, Technical Director and Lord of Funk, The Mandebrot Set

Examine your recruitment policies. How do you select people for a job? How can you include creativity in the specification? This should be considered at two levels. First, is the individual open to the idea of innovation? Do they resist change, even if it is well founded? Do they have a positive understanding of why creativity is important. Second, are they particularly creative individuals? Look at this from a number of directions. Puzzle-solving is not always an effective guide, as many creative people get bored very quickly with puzzles. A puzzle is external, whereas creativity is essentially internal. Try describing a business scenario and ask them to come up with creative ways forward. Creativity should not be your sole criterion, though acceptance of creativity has to be high on your list. Creative ability is less essential, as anyone's innate creativity can be improved using techniques and practice, but recruiting for a high level of creativity is a good way to seed the company and accelerate the process of creative reform.

Making a start

'Innovation is the central issue in economic prosperity.' *Michael Porter, Harvard Business School*

The agenda items are fearsome – taking on innovation is not a minor task – but many of the items (or at least the preparation for them) can be taken on immediately. Do not put off the establishment of a creativity culture – there may not be time to do it later. Remember the need for output discipline when being creative. Set some difficult but attainable deadlines for getting the creativity agenda items under way and complete. The most important thing, though is to make a start. Many companies will never do it – and there is your competitive advantage, because your company will.

If you have taken this book seriously, you will be on the way to implementing an agenda for creativity. The outcome will be significant changes to you company culture, your organization and the way you interact with your staff. These changes are neither frivolous nor tinkering in response to a fad, but are changes for the sake of survival – and a better working environment too. Creativity should be, and can be a win-win-win-win situation for the company, the management, the staff and the customers. Make sure that you reap the benefits.

Executive summary

- Cultural change is the prime mover.
- Suggestion schemes and reward schemes are good starting points.
- Training both in managing innovation and being creative is essential.
- Examining and building creative resources should be an early activity.
- Do not put off making a start.

Chapter 10

Finding out more

Innovation sources

This book is a taster of the potential that creativity has to enhance a business. It may be enough, but should you wish to delve further, there is a whole range of resources available to both enhance your creativity skills and provide direct support for innovation.

The Internet

The Internet provides a growing range of sources of information on business creativity. While addresses change with remarkable frequency, the suggestions below will provide up-to-date links to background information, techniques, software and more.

http://www.cul.co.uk – Creativity Unleashed Limited: general information, free and shareware software, creativity books, links to other sites and more.

http://www.ozemail.com.au/~caveman/creative – The Australian creativity page. Reflecting the strong interest in creativity in Australia, this is a comprehensive collection of information, book and software reviews. Heavily influenced by Edward de Bono's work.

http://www.waterw.com/~lucia/awlinks.html – Lucia's Creativity Links. A highly eclectic set of links which include everything from serious business creativity to the strangest alternative thinking.

Books

Books on creativity vary widely in approach from the purely theoretical to the pragmatic business text. While it is possible to get all that is needed to make innovation flourish in business from the business books, it can be helpful to understand a little more of the underlying process, hence the academic recommendations.

There are few things less helpful than a long, uninformative list of every possible book. Instead, this list concentrates on some key texts, and provides some information about each volume.

Like all ephemeral resources, books come and go. A more up-to-date book source is the business creativity section of the Creativity Unleashed on-line bookshop. See **http://www.cul.co.uk/books** for more detail.

Theory

Applied Imaginations, **Alex Osborn (Charles Scribner's Sons, 1963)**
Osborn's seminal text that started the business creativity bandwagon rolling. Out of print at the time of publication.

The Act of Creation, **Arthur Koestler (Penguin Arkana, 1989)**
Koestler's thick tome does take a little working through, but it defines the nature of creativity and the principles of making creativity happen in a way that has rarely been achieved before or since.

Water Logic, **Edward de Bono (Viking, 1993)**
Innovation requires a move from the traditional view of what something is, to a more flexible of view of what it might result in. Such an approach, referred to by de Bono as 'Water Logic', is the basis for this volume. Useful not so much for the 'practical' concept of flowscapes as the understanding of the difference between perception and traditional logic. If unavailable, try de Bono's *I am Right, You are Wrong* (Viking, 1990), which explores much of the same territory.

Practical business

Imagination Engineering, **Paul Birch and Brian Clegg (Pitman Publishing, 1996)**
Probably the best single volume for bringing an individual or group up to speed on practical business creativity. Puts creativity techniques into an easy-to-use framework to make them more appropriate to the business environment. Combines practical techniques with stretching exercises and short fictional 'tale pieces' which push the reader into a different mode of thinking.

Serious Creativity, **Edward de Bono (HarperCollins, 1996)**
De Bono's clearest and most concise summary of his creativity theories and techniques. Begins with an explanation of the need for creativity, goes on to introduce tools and techniques and finishes with practical application. Pulls together the content of several of his other books.

A Whack on the Side of the Head, **Roger von Oech (Warner Books, 1983)**
Von Oech, Silicon Valley's favourite creativity guru meanders through the

blockages to creativity and how to unblock them in a fun presentation which is light without being lightweight.

A Kick in the Seat of the Pants, **Roger von Oech (HarperCollins, 1986)**
Von Oech expands the 'A Whack on the Side of the Head' approach to include four primary approaches to creativity, each with their own strengths and contributions. Again written in a very light, fun style, though slightly less easy to digest than its predecessor.

The Creative Whack Pack, **Roger van Oech (US Games Systems, 1989)**
Puts the techniques of *A Kick in the Seat of the Pants* in a flexible card pack, ideal for group use.

Jamming: the Art and Discipline of Business Creativity, **John Kao (Harper-Collins, 1996)**
The US creativity guru who best spans academia and practical business, Kao's *Jamming* takes the metaphor of jazz as a starting point for looking at creativity in business. His approach of creativity auditing will find favour with those who like scorecards, although some find the jazz metaphor is stretched excessively.

Managing 'Live' Innovation, **Michel Syrett and Jean Lammiman (Butter-worth-Heinemann, 1998)**
Although not packed with practical measures, this is an extremely useful text on the atmosphere and direction required for encouraging innovation to flourish in a company.

Instant Creativity, **Brian Clegg and Paul Birch (Kogan Page, 1999)**
Instant Teamwork, **Brian Clegg and Paul Birch (Kogan Page, 1998)**
Instant Creativity is a source book of creativity techniques, ready to apply at a moment's notice. Unlike most of the other titles above, it does not attempt to put the techniques into context or a framework, but simply provides a bag of techniques. The companion volume, *Instant Teamwork* contains warm-up and time-out exercises, which are ideal for providing a creativity boost to an individual or to a group.

Organizing creatively

DisOrganization, **Brian Clegg and Paul Birch (FT Pitman Publishing, 1998)**
DisOrganization is the complete guide to reorganizing a company around innovative lines. Dismissing compromise as inappropriate for survival in the new, frantic world of business, it proposes adopting apparently contradictory extremes – fragmentation and centralization, reaction and innovation, management and leadership.

The Empty Raincoat, **Charles Handy (Arrow, 1995)**
Handy's typically philosophical approach turns the traditional company-centred view on its head, putting the individual at the core of business philosophy.

The Tom Peters Seminar – Crazy Times call for Crazy Organizations, **Tom Peters (Macmillan, 1994)**
The ever ebullient Tom Peters calls for a totally different organizational focus, driven by an entrepreneurial focus on superb customer service and the wider network.

A different viewpoint

The Corporate Fool, **David Firth and Alan Leigh (Capstone, 1998)**
An examination of the corporate jester and other applications of foolery in business.

The Dilbert Principle, **Scott Adams (Boxtree, 1996)**
The Dilbert Future, **Scott Adams (Boxtree, 1997)**
The unparalleled cartoonist of business and computing brings his wit and creativity to make improving business a delight.

Still Further Up the Organization, **Robert Townsend (Simon and Schuster, 1990)**
The one-time president and chairman of Avis brings a lifetime of business experience to point out what's wrong with business in a very enjoyable way. Latest in a series of books in which Townsend has refined and expanded his vision of what is wrong with business.

Setting the context

In Chapter 7 we looked at the fit of creativity with a number of other management skills. While these are secondary to the subject of this book, this short list will provide a starting point for further reading.

Competitive Advantage, **Michael Porter (Free Press, 1998)**
A brilliant exploration of the forces of competition by the business guru who has made it his hallmark.

Honing Your Knowledge Skills, **Mariana Funes and Nancy Johnson (Butterworth-Heinemann, 1998)**
An introduction to the people side of knowledge management.

Managing with the Power of NLP, **David Molden (Pitman Publishing, 1996)**
An application-oriented book on neuro-linguistic programming.

Understand Neuro-Linguistic Programming in a Week, **Mo Shapiro (Hodder and Stoughton, 1998)**
A concise introduction to neuro-linguistic programming.

Other references

The books listed here are not specifically recommended reading to find out more about business creativity, but are referred to in the text in addition to some of the books previously listed.

Cognitive Psychology. Thinking and Creating, J. R. Hayes (Dorsey Press, 1978).
Creating the Digital Future, Albert Yu (Free Press, 1998)
The Five Day Course in Thinking, Edward de Bono (Pelican, 1969)
Hare Brain and Tortoise Mind, Guy Claxton (Fourth Estate, 1997)
Lateral Thinking, Edward de Bono (Penguin, 1990)
The Psychology of Thought, D. M. Johnson (Harper and Row, 1955)
Six Thinking Hats, Edward de Bono (Penguin, 1990)
Six Action Shoes, Edward de Bono (Fontana, 1993)

Training and consultancy

Creativity is something that is often required in a hurry, without the need for extensive study. It is also a discipline which is much easier to put across by demonstration than by description. Many creativity techniques sound odd – it is not surprising, as this is the business of uncommon sense. It is entirely possible to build creativity and innovation in a company without outside help, but there is no doubt that the quickest way to get started is by bringing in expertise, either to provide training or to facilitate creativity sessions directly.

A number of companies specialize in this kind of consultancy:

Creative Dimensions
1 Southfield
Aldbourne
Marlborough
Wiltshire SN8 2DY
Email: blincoln@zetnet.co.uk
Telephone: 01672 540359

Creativity Unleashed
The Thicket
Upper Wanborough
Wiltshire SN4 0DQ
Website: http://www.cul.co.uk
E-mail: info@cul.co.uk
Telephone and fax: 01793 791393

Runston Consulting
Runston Farm,
Shirenewton,
Monmouthshire NP6 6LS
E-mail: Paul_S_Birch@msn.com
Telephone: 01291 420301
Fax: 01291 423546

Theory B
Prospect House,
Sovereign Street,
Leeds LS1 4BJ
E-mail: janine@theoryb.com
Telephone: 0113 244 9499
Fax: 0113 237 1095

Index

ABB, 51
Academics, 9
Act of Creation, The, 10
Action checklists, 76–8
Adams, Mark, 10, 61, 88
Adams, Scott, 31, 54
Advertising, 67
Agenda for innovation, 92
Analysis, 14
Answers, generating, 20, 73
Arguments against creativity, 63
Artificial intelligence, 82, 85
Artist, 1, 13
Assessment, creativity, 37, 95
Audit of creativity, 75, 77

BAA, 19
Bacon, Francis, 58
Balloons, 59
Barnevik, Percy, 51
Beaven, James, 67
Bell, Alexander Graham, 59
Benetton, 3
Berry, Henry, 18, 30, 49
Beyond techniques, 28
Biography, business, 31
Birch, Paul, 31, 40, 49–51, 66
Birth of creativity, 8
Blockages to creativity, 13
BMW, 55
Bok, Chan, 8
Books, access to, 41, 100
Brainstorming, 9, 26, 68
Brands, 68
Branson, Richard, 96
British Airways, 40, 54
Budget for innovation, 96
Building on ideas, 25
Buildings, 52–5

Bulletin boards, 26, 27, 44
Burke, Edmund, 50
Business processes, 24, 33, 45–7, 82
Business process re-engineering, 82
Business skills, 83

Campbell, Ian, 16, 47
Campbell, Joseph, 5
Car parking, 19
Carroll, Lewis, 2
Case studies, about, 74
CBI, 40
Celebrating success, 94
Centres, innovation, 41, 99
Chain of command, 34
Change, 2
Charles, Jacques, 59
Checklists for action, 76–8
Chessboard, 18
Children, 11
Claxton, Guy, 28
Clegg, Brian, 31, 49–51
Coaching, 97
Coca-Cola, 34, 75
Cognitive Psychology, 18
Communication:
    between layers, 34
    open, 34
Computer modelling, 80
Computers, 26
Concessionaires, 19
Consistency of service, 68
Consultants, 38, 39, 100, 104
Context, 79
Corporate jester, 40
CoRT, 12
Covey, Stephen, 85
Creating the Digital Future, 34
Creative organization, 50–2, 97, 98

Creativity:
  agenda, 92
  audit, 75
  budget, 96
  centres, 41, 99
  culture, 32, 61, 70, 72, 77, 93
  Forum, the, 13
  future of, 83
  groups, 41
  manager, 41
  powerhouses, 30
  resources, 37–45, 100, 101
  rewarding, 36, 37
  software, 27, 45, 85, 101
  sources, 30, 103
  systematic, 70, 78
  techniques, 10, 17, 20, 33, 46, 68, 69,
     84, 100
Cross-functional teams, 66
Culture of creativity, 32, 61, 70, 72, 77,
   93
Customer service, 69

Darwin, Charles, 25
Deadlines, 35
de Bono, Edward, 11–13, 17
Decision making, 14, 66
Differentiation, 31
Dilbert, 31
Directions for innovation, 83
Discipline, 35
DisOrganization, 35, 49–51, 83
Doherty, Catherine, 68
Doing nothing, 19, 98
Dos and don'ts , 72
Dumigan, Peter, 92

Edison, Thomas, 20
Education, 12
Einstein, Albert, 9, 98
Electronic mail, 26, 27, 42, 43, 100
Electronic resources, 41
E-mail, *see* Electronic mail
Emerson, Ralph Waldo, 62
Empty Raincoat, The, 89
Encyclopaedia, 27
Evaluating ideas, 22, 73
Evaluation, premature, 9, 17
Experience, 14

Expert systems, 86
Explorer, 13
Exploring the problem, 18, 73
Expo 2000, 62

Facilitators, 38, 39, 100, 104
Facilities management, 69
Fantasy, 21
Ferrandis, José, 39, 99
Filtering ideas, 9
Finance departments, 69
Firth, David, 33, 100
Five Day Course in Thinking, The, 11
Forecasting, 66
Four stages, 18
Framework for creativity, 18, 31
French and Raven, 47
Fry, Art, 48
Fulfilment ratio, 75, 76
Funes and Johnson, 86
Future of creativity, 83

Generating answers, 20, 73
Gifts as reward, 95
Gonzalez-Regueral, Adriano, 22
Gordon, Bill, 31
Groups, 25, 41
Gurus:
  business, 31, 83
  creativity, 10
Gyroscope, 3

Handy, Charles, 31, 50, 83, 89
Hare Brain and Tortoise Mind, 28
Harvard Business School, 2, 30
Hats, six thinking, 11, 12
Hayes, J. R., 18
Heathrow Airport, 19
Hill climbing, 14
Hiring for innovation, 32, 47
Homeopathy, 22
Honing Your Knowledge Skills, 86
Human resources, 69
Humour, 31, 40

ICL, 34
Idea:
  generation, 20, 24, 28, 45, 73
  quotient, 75, 76

Ideas, building on, 25
Ideas Olympics, 62, 94
Identifying the question , 18, 73
Ignoring creativity, 32
Imagination engineering, 31
Immediacy, 42
Implementation, 23, 35, 74
Impresario, 49
Individuals, 25
Information technology, 26, 69, 84
In-house magazine, 93
Innovation:
  agenda, 92
  audit, 75
  budget, 96
  centres, 41, 99
  culture, 32, 61, 70, 72, 77, 93
  Forum, the, 13
  future of, 83
  groups, 41
  manager, 41
  powerhouses, 30
  resources, 37–45, 100, 101
  rewarding, 36, 37
  software, 27, 45, 85, 101
  sources, 30, 103
  systematic, 70, 78
  techniques, 10, 17, 20, 33, 46, 68, 69,
    84, 100
Input, 35
Institutionalizing innovation , 93
Intel, 34, 35
Internalization of creativity, 28, 84
Internet, 26, 27, 44, 101, 104
Internet commerce, 74
Intranets, 34, 44, 100
Intuition, 66
IT, *see* Information technology

Jakubowicz, Dr Helmut, 44
Jazz, 30
Jester, 1, 40
Johnson, D. M., 18
Josephson, Professor Brian, 22
Judge, 13
Judging ideas, 9, 17
Justice systems, 11

Kao, John, 30, 49, 75

Kick in the Seat of the Pants, A, 13
Knowledge:
  engineers, 86,
  management, 81, 82,
  unconscious, 9
Knowledge-based systems, 86
Koestler, Arthur, 1, 10
Kolind, Lars, 52
Kvaerner, 62

Lateral thinking, 11
Lateral Thinking, 11
Layers, communication between, 34
Leadership, 49, 96, 97
League tables, school, 76
Levitt, Theodore, 2
Light sabre, 43
Lincoln, Brian, 38
Locke, John, 57
Logic, 80, 82
Lotus Notes, 44, 101
Louis XVI, 59

Malcolm, Bob, 26, 93
Management, 49, 96, 97
Managing 'Live' Innovation, 49, 55, 83
Manchester Business School, 31
Maps, 5
  by chapter, 7
  by concept, 6
  mind, 45
Market risk, 91
Marketing, 67
Mars, 95
Marshall, Sir Colin, 40
Matchmaker, 19
May, Phil, 89
Mechanics of innovation, 16
Mechanisms of power, 47
Media Lab, MIT, 30
Metaphor, 21
Michalko, Michael, 3, 68
Microscope, electron, 59
Microsoft, 85
Mind maps, 45
Mini-company, 51
Misdirection, 17
Misunderstanding, 59
Modifying the problem, 20

Monitoring implementation, 75, 76
Montgolfier brothers, 59
Morland, D. Verne, 40
Morris, Peter J., 38, 41, 65, 101

Netcompany, 51
Neural networks, 86
Neuro-linguistic programming, 81, 82
New products and services, 24
Nicholas, Alex, 28
NLP, *see* Neuro-linguisting
   programming
Notes, Lotus, 44
Nothing, doing, 19, 98

Oates, Keith, 79
Objectives, 49
Obstacles, 19
Obstacles to creativity, 13
Olympics, Ideas, 62
Open communications, 34
Operational research, 80
Operations, 68
Opportunities from creativity 88
OR, *see* Operational research
Organizational boundaries, 66
Organizations:
   creative, 50–2, 69, 97, 98,
   hierarchical, 34, 83
Origins of creativity, 8
Osborn, Alex, 9, 17
Oticon, 52
Outcome, polishing, 22
Output, 35
Outsourcing, 69

Patterson, Julian, 52, 65, 88
Pauling, Linus, 23
Perception, 58
Performance-based pay, 94
Peters, Tom, 1, 31, 50, 79, 80, 83, 92
Physical environment, 52
Pinstriped creativity, 12
Planning, 23
Polishing the outcome, 22, 73
Pop culture, 13
Porter, Michael, 102
Positioning creativity, 24
Post-it Notes, 48, 65

Power, mechanisms of, 47
Powerhouse, innovation, 30
PR, 68
Practical, making ideas, 23
Prince, George, 31
Principles, 49
Problem rephrasing, 18, 20
Problem solving, 14, 20, 24, 28, 45, 69,
   73, 80
Processes, business, 24, 33, 45–7, 82, 98
Process re-engineering, 82
Products, new, 24, 68
Projects, starting, 24
Prototyping, 23
Psychology, 10
Psychology of Thought, The, 18
Purchasing, 69
Pygmalion technology, 57–9, 65

Quality control, 76
Question, identifying the, 18, 19, 73

Ralf, Mark, 70, 83
Random stimulation, 21
Rapley, Keith, 4
Reality check, 74
Recognition, 36, 37
Recruiting for creativity, 32, 47, 101
Re-engineering business processes , 82
Refining ideas, 22, 73
Regular sessions, 25
Reis, Johann, 59
Rephrasing the problem, 18, 73
Resources, innovation, 37–45, 78, 100,
   101
Rewarding innovation, 36, 37, 94–6
Rickards, Tudor, 14, 31, 97
Right answer, single, 12
Risk, 66, 91
Risk taking, 34
Ruscoe, John, 34

Sage, 1
Sales, 67
School league tables, 76
Schools, creativity in, 12
Selection of ideas, 22
Selection of staff, 102
Self patterning systems, 17, 82

Selling creativity, 62, 70, 77, 91
Selling results, 65
Serious Creativity, 11
Services, new, 24
Shared space, 52–5
Shaw, George Bernard, 35
Sigmoid curve, 89, 90
Simulation, 80
Singer, Spence, 48
Six thinking hats, 11, 12
Sleight of hand, 17
Smokestacks, 66
Software, creativity, 27, 45, 85, 101
Sources of creativity, 30, 103
Space, shared, 52–5
Spellchecker, 26
Stanford University, 30
Starting a project, 24
Statistics, 80
Status quo, 75
Stimulating creativity, 27
Strategy, 24, 66
Strengths of creativity, 88
Subculture, 41
Suggestion schemes, 60, 61, 93, 94
Support sections, 69
Suppressing creativity, 9
Svendsen, David, 32
SWOT analysis, 88
Symptoms, 18
Synectics, 31
Syrett and Lammiman, 49, 55, 83
Systematic creativity, 70, 78
Systems, self-patterning, 17

Teams, 25, 66
Techniques, 10, 17, 20, 33, 46, 68, 69, 84, 100
Technology risk, 91

Telephone, 59
Teleworking, 52–5
Text 100, 68
Theory B, 30
Therapists, 81
Thesaurus, 26
Threats from creativity, 90
3M, 48, 65
Time, wasted, 44
Tom Peters Seminar, The, 79, 92
Total quality management, 34, 80
Townsend, Robert, 31
Toyota, 62
TQM, see Total quality management
Training, 39, 41, 77, 99, 100, 104
Trust, 83
Tzu, Sun, 45

Uncommon sense, 21, 22
Unconscious knowledge, 9, 28

Venture capitalists, 91
von Oech, Roger, 13

War stories, about, 74
Warrior, 13
Wasted time, 44
Water, structure of, 22
Weaknesses of creativity, 88
Whack on the Side of the Head, A, 13
Whack Pack, Creative, 14
White, Jeremy N., 24
Wolff, Michael, 90
World Wide Web, 26, 27, 44, 101, 104
Why, asking, 19

Yu, Dr Albert, 34

Zen creativity , 28